DO YOU KNOW THE DIFFERENCE BETWEEN THE TRUE AND THE FALSE IN SEX?

A woman who prefers the missionary position likes to play patsy for men.

A man who lets a woman get astride him is essentially passive.

Couples who assume the spoon position have something amiss in their relationship.

Simultaneous orgasm is the goal of good sex.

A sexually healthy woman seeks multiple orgasms.

Cocaine heightens sexual activity and pleasure.

Making a sexual fantasy come true is the way to the heights of ecstasy.

You may <u>think</u> you know everything about a loving sexual relationship, but after you read this revealing book, you will know that you know all that you can and should about intimacy, spontaneity, physicality, commitment, and pleasure in your partner's and your—

LOVELIVES

"ENLIGHTENING!"

—PUBLISHERS WEEKLY

HOW WE MAKE LOVE

SAMUEL DUNKELL, M.D.

ILLUSTRATED WITH
68 SEX POSITIONS

A SIGNET BOOK

For Ruth

SIGNET
Published by the Penguin Group
Penguin Books USA Inc., 375 Hudson Street,
New York, New York 10014, U.S.A.
Penguin Books Ltd, 27 Wrights Lane,
London W8 5TZ, England
Penguin Books Australia Ltd, Ringwood,
Victoria, Australia
Penguin Books Canada Ltd, 2801 John Street,
Markham, Ontario, Canada L3R 1B4
Penguin Books (N.Z.) Ltd, 182-190 Wairau Road,
Auckland 10, New Zealand

Penguin Books Ltd, Registered Offices:
Harmondsworth, Middlesex, England

Published by Signet, an imprint of New American Library,
a division of Penguin Books USA Inc.

This is an authorized reprint of a hardcover edition published by
William Morrow and Company, Inc.

First Signet Printing, January, 1980
13 12 11 10 9 8 7 6 5

Drawings by Ruth Dunkell

 REGISTERED TRADEMARK—MARCA REGISTRADA

Printed in the United States of America

Contents

CHAPTER 1

CHAPTER 1

The Faces of Love and Sex

> Her arms do lend his neck a sweet embrace; In-
> corporate then they seem; face grows to face.
>
> WILLIAM SHAKESPEARE,
> *Venus and Adonis*

The sexual act may be described from a myriad of
different perspectives, ranging from the sublimely poetic to the coldly clinical. The poet may seek to convey its ecstasy, emphasizing the emotional coloration
of the act. The scientist's approach may be a detached, abstractly biological one, stressing the genetic,
the physiological, the anatomical, or the neurological
aspects of sex. Others may be interested in statistical
overviews, searching for behavioral norms; like Kinsey, they may conduct interviews and surveys to determine how many people prefer particular sexual
activities and how often they indulge in them. Cross-
cultural anthropological studies, such as Margaret
Mead's and Bronislaw Malinowski's essays on the
peoples of primitive (Stone Age) cultures, seek to
make clear the relationship among sexual practices,
temperament, and the broader structure of particular
societies. The anthropological and the poetic may be
combined, as in Paolo Mantegazza's pioneering 1885
work *The Sexual Relations of Mankind*.

Mantegazza's work made him in a sense one of the
founders of the modern field of sexology. Other major founding figures, writing at the turn of the century, were Richard von Krafft-Ebing, Albert Moll,
Havelock Ellis, and Magnus Hirschfeld. Greatly influenced by the Darwinian theory of evolution, they
viewed impotence, premature ejaculation, and sexual
"deviations" as evidence of a constitutional weakness

1

associated with hereditary degeneration. They believed this degeneration to have been caused by alco-
holism or—in true Victorian style—excessive masturbation! Eventually this basically biological and theo-
retically rather hazy approach to sexuality gave way
to other more comprehensive and subtle concepts.

The freudian psychoanalytic approach focused
more directly on the individual's particular life history, although there were still some constitutional
elements involved. In the freudian approach the
individual's sexual destiny was dominated by an un-
derlying sexual drive. This drive was believed to be
fueled by biological energies and shaped by the vicis-
situdes of psychic development existing in successive
stages of oral, anal, and genital fixation. While Freud,
through his brilliant insights, succeeded in dispelling
many myths about sexuality, he also created some of
his own—such as the idea that women were innately
passive. Later psychoanalytic thinkers revised Freud's
approaches to love and sexuality, producing such clas-
sics as Erich Fromm's *The Art of Loving* and the
works of Theodore Reik and Medard Boss.

Recently Masters and Johnson have given us the
clearest understanding yet of the realities of physical
sexual response through a host of clinical laboratory
investigations. Their techniques for combating sexual
dysfunction have been combined with a stress on the
importance of communications between partners and
how these can influence sexual performance.

Because human sexuality is so immensely complex,
it can be validly approached from many angles. The
biologist speaks of hormones and erectile tissue, the
anthropologist of cultural determinants, and the poet
of love. But how does each of us as an individual *experience* this complexity? Each of us is a biological
entity, each of us comes from a particular cultural
background, and each of us seeks love. All these factors enter into the totality of sex. Sex and love do not
in actuality exist in isolation from one another but are

related as a drop of water is to rain. We can analyze the properties of a drop of water, defining its chemical makeup, yet this will give us no insight into the palpable experience of being caught in a spring shower, nor explain why rain gives us pleasure on one occasion and irritates us on another. Similarly, an analysis of the congestion of the pelvic blood vessels during intercourse cannot convey anything about the experiencing of sexual ecstasy or enlighten us as to why coitus with a beloved partner gives us a joy we fail to discover with a casual pickup.

In this book I shall be viewing human sexuality within my own very special framework, the *phenomenological* approach. To help in understanding this point of view, let us look first at an example from a nonsexual area. Suppose that a person is suffering from a sprained back. To the doctor who treats this back pain, it is the muscular, ligamentous, and bony structures of the back that are paramount. On the basis of his experience and his knowledge of orthopedics, the physician will determine the advisability of a back brace or make a judgment that exercise, and the application of heat and massage will be sufficient. But for the experiencing individual, the suffering person with the sprained back, there is an additional dimension—what a back injury actually means in terms of one's life. Every time an attempt is made to stand up and walk there will be tension and pain. Upon getting out of bed in the morning, the person may find it takes an hour or two before it is possible to stand fully erect. Only small steps can be taken when walking. Thus, the ability to move about in life is curtailed. Phenomenologically, the ongoing movement of one's very existence has been hobbled.

This book deals with the phenomenology of sex. My concern will be with the lived dimension of sex— going beyond the physiology of the sexual organs, the mechanics of the sexual act, or the stages of the sexual response cycle. All these matters will be considered, but in terms of the individual's whole existence. A young male patient of mine, for example, prefers to have intercourse in the rear-approach position; he insists on inserting his penis into his wife's vagina from behind her. In discussing this position, he alluded to a mild claustrophobia from which he suffers, experiencing anxiety when he is in a closed elevator, for instance. He states that the reason he prefers the rear-entry position is that it makes him less conscious of being closed in than would be true with the face-to-face position. Rear entry allows him a perceptual openness with respect to his environment. By kneeling on the bed, he is able to keep his torso and head upright, still involved in a world of extended horizons and able to see all around him. It should be emphasized that the importance of the open horizon to this man is reflected in many areas of his life. He dislikes umbrellas, whether in the rain or at the beach, because they cut off his view of the world around him. Thus we can see that his insistence on a particular sex position is not simply a matter of sexual peculiarity, but rather an extension of his general approach to the world.

My patient's wife does not object to his choice of a sex position. She does not feel the need for face-to-face contact that another woman might find important. If she did feel that need strongly, it would obviously introduce an additional element of conflict into this couple's sexual relationship.

In a couple relationship, each of the partners is an individual. Each has a particular identity. We know that every human being has characteristic ways of behaving, of meeting the world, of living. But we do not always recognize the extent to which these identifying characteristic ways of behaving show themselves in all areas of life, in work, in social interaction, in love relationships. What is more, this set of characteristics is visibly delineated in how people physically move through the world, how they react in a bodily way to their environment; even their sleep positions, as demonstrated in my previous book, carry the unmistakable stamp of their particular ways of living.

During sexual intercourse the congruence between our emotional ways of living and our bodily ways of being is particularly vivid and intense. The erect penis, the tumescent clitoris, the stiffened nipples all reflect the emotional engorgement that we feel. If we have anxiety concerning the sexual encounter, however, our bodies will reflect that. A man may have difficulty in achieving or sustaining an erection and effecting penetration; a woman's vagina, instead of being open and lubricious, may remain tight and dry.

In experiencing sex, we are intrinsically in touch with our own feelings and responses. Yet at the same time our world is shared with another human being. From the moment of birth we live in a world of others, but it is during intercourse that our own special world is most completely conjoined with the world of another. A loving sexual relationship carries with it a need for each partner to deal with five distinct elements: intimacy, spontaneity, physicality, commitment, and pleasure. Each individual's feelings about these five elements will be different, and in a particular individual one or more of these elements may be a cause of stress or anxiety. The stress may arise from a person's social standards, his or her personal history, his or her degree of sexual experience, or a combination of such factors. And when anxiety is felt, all individuals utilize special measures—in keeping with their general way of meeting the world—to ward off the stress.

If a person fears intimacy, for instance, he or she will adopt patterns of lovemaking that shield the self from full openness. If spontaneity is difficult for a person to achieve in other areas of existence, so in the sexual act that person's approach is likely to be carefully contained, clinging to a set routine that makes surprise unlikely. If an individual is upset by physicality itself, by body contact, by interpenetration, then sexual relations will probably be considerably constricted. A fear of commitment will be shown not only in the person's overall way of treating the love partner but also in the very alignment of the body during sex. And if a person is afraid of pleasure, of sensory gratification, another characteristic set of defenses will be erected. Each of these elements—intimacy, spontaneity, physicality, commitment, and pleasure—has an effect on the chosen love positions and patterns of sexual behavior of the individual, and I will be discussing these effects throughout this book.

When facing a situation that they feel demands some precaution, human beings draw upon an immense variety of modalities and stratagems to ease their anxiety. The person who fears spontaneity may indeed be able to achieve it in the course of making love. But before one lets go, before one takes the leap into the unknown territory of intimacy and pleasure, certain characteristic attitudes and modes of behavior will usually be assumed as takeoff postures. These postures will reflect to a certain extent the special ways that individual has of meeting the stress of events encountered in daily life. Three different people will enter the cold water of a swimming pool in three different ways. One may do it inch by inch, climbing backward down the ladder at the side of the pool. Another may wade in the shallow end, getting wet to the waist and then dunking the rest of the body in a sudden submersion. The third will dive in bravely from the springboard. And each of these three people is likely to adopt similar individual precautionary techniques in entering into those areas of a sexual relationship about which they might feel a degree of chill uncertainty.

It is important to recognize that the defensive or security-inducing postural alignments, attitudes, and stratagems that are assumed by the individual are made use of not only at the beginning of the sexual encounter but throughout it. Coitus is commonly agreed to consist of four phases: the arousal phase, the plateau phase, the orgasmic phase, and the resolution phase. Since orgasm is the moment of greatest abandonment in sex, it requires the most intense marshaling of one's characteristic coping patterns if the individual is to feel secure enough to let go fully. Sexual problems, such as premature ejaculation in the male or orgasmic dysfunction in the female, are often indicative of "plateau anxiety." With such anxiety, the individual cannot achieve sufficient security to enter fully and freely into the total sexual experience, cannot make the smooth ascendant leap from the plateau phase to the orgasmic phase.

The need to prepare oneself when making an ascent to another plane or phase operates in all areas of life. It can be seen very clearly with patients in psychotherapy. In most cases, when patients take a significant step forward in their development, opening up new world possibilities that they had previously been unable to handle or maintain, we find that they experience anxiety and as a result resist the forward step. To deal with the anxiety, each person will make use of a characteristic pattern of security behavior in an effort to forestall the attempted growth into the future. Experienced analysts know, therefore, that there is no development without anxiety and resistance.

A young female patient of mine, for instance, will periodically show symptoms of feeling that the world and she are unreal, that everything is bleak and empty, fearsome and threatening—and she will lament her difficulties and her hopelessness. But at this point we both know that she is about to take a significant step forward and is girding herself against the stress of making it. By expressing hopelessness, she is taking out insurance against failure in the move forward: If everything is hopeless, then making a change cannot matter, and if it doesn't matter, she need not fear the possibility of failure. In the sexual arena a similar stratagem can be seen at work in the case of a young woman who was reared in an extremely puritanical family. When she is on the verge of orgasm, this young woman often calls out, "I mustn't, I mustn't," thus "paying her respects" to her family background and freeing herself to experience the pleasure of orgasm.

The question arises: Is every sex-love encounter somewhat anxiety-provoking? Certainly, anxiety is basic to the human condition. We do not usually know what will happen next, and therefore we are always to some degree anxious about the future. But the anxiety we feel in respect to the unknown is not necessarily a reason for depression or fear. For an actor waiting to walk onstage, a chef preparing an important dinner, or an executive facing a crucial business meeting, a certain degree of anxiety can act as a tonic, mobilizing the adrenaline and causing the person to perform his or her role at a higher level of awareness, to meet the situation with the best that one has to offer.

The man and woman who initially dislike one another but fall in love when they are placed together in a dangerous situation is a staple plot device of novels and films. But such behavior is not merely a fantasy of fiction writers; it is a demonstrable aspect of human psychology in general. Stanley Schachter of Columbia University has shown in an important series of experiments that when people are made anxious in an experimental situation, they tend to affiliate themselves strongly with those suffering a similar anxiety. Schachter's attribution theory has been used as the basis for other experiments demonstrating that anxiety can cause an increase in sexual arousal. In an experiment by Donald Dutton and Arthur Aron at the University of British Columbia, two groups of randomly chosen men were tested. One group crossed a high, swaying suspension bridge, and the other group a much lower and more stable one. As they reached the other side, the men in both groups were met by an attractive young woman who interviewed them. She also gave them her phone number in case they wished to discuss the experiment further. In answering the questionnaire, the men who had crossed the dangerous suspension bridge gave replies that had a higher sexual content than those of the other group, and more of them tried to contact the female interviewer later on.

Poets and philosophers have always been acutely concerned with the anxiety that accompanies sexual love. Perhaps the most eloquent monograph on the subject is Stendhal's *On Love*. Stendhal accentuates the dual nature of the love experience: The lover, with a surge of joy and hope, idealizes his beloved, yet immediately feels a tremor of anxiety and doubt. As Stendhal saw it, the lover always swims between the blissful security felt in the presence of the beloved and the anxiety that arises from the awareness that complete certainty is not possible in human experience. Yet the doubt and uncertainty, even as they cause anxiety, seem to increase the tension that always exists in the love relationship, heightening the pleasure when affirmation or reaffirmation of love actually occurs. Without the uncertainty the ultimate pleasure would be less.

The current attempt to remove the uncertainty and tension from sexual experience by reducing it to a question of mechanics and techniques—a mere technological process to be mastered—seeks to ward off the element of the unknown in sex and love. Yet it is precisely the opportunity to enter into "unknown modes of being," in Wordsworth's phrase, that makes a profound sex-love experience so moving and so satisfying. I believe that if the sex-love encounter is to be emotionally meaningful, there must be some degree of abandonment, a moving into the unknown. In an ongoing couple relationship, the most exciting sexual episodes are the unprogrammed ones, in which the greatest degree of spontaneity and concomitant uncertainty exists. When that spontaneity and that sense of entering into the unknown are missing, the sense of being transported beyond oneself will be lessened.

Anxiety is thus inevitably and properly a part of the sex-love condition. Each of us, in dealing with that anxiety, will draw upon our same security patterns and attitudes that we use to deal with the rest of our encounters with life's uncertainties—security patterns that show our basic attitudes toward life. Those attitudes are reflected not just in our words and deeds but in the very movement of our bodies. Just as the face-down, spread-out position of the prone sleeper illustrates an attempt to keep a maximum amount of the sleep world under control and organized, just as the opposite position of the back sleeper shows a person's receptivity to the phenomena of the world, so the uses that we make of our bodies during sex reflect our general tendencies in meeting stress and uncertainty. In later chapters I will be spelling out in detail the ways in which we use our characteristic defenses in our sexual relationships. But there is another equally important aspect to our sexual lives that makes it possible for us to transcend our anxieties, to reach beyond ourselves and enter into a special unity with our partners in love. Before we can fully understand the psychological significance of the sex positions and patterns we choose for ourselves, we must begin by recognizing that sexual relations take place within the context of a *love world*. It is the qualities of that love world that I will be defining in the next chapter.

CHAPTER 2

The Love World

From birth on, human beings have an absolute need to touch and be touched. The infantile-dependency research studies of the American psychoanalyst Rene Spitz demonstrate that when infants do not have considerable affectionate touching and holding as part of their early developmental stages, a characteristic depression sets in that can lead to marasmus—a state of extreme malnutrition. In some cases the untouched, unheld child simply gives up and dies. To be held and touched is the only way that the infant can gain the knowledge that it is loved. As the child grows, it will begin to try to express its own love in return, reaching out to touch others.

The eroticism of the skin, therefore, is not merely a matter of physical arousal but is fundamentally connected with our need to love and be loved. All of us seek the touch of love. We all seek to hold and be held by another human being, not just because it "feels good" and is pleasurable but because to engage in sexual intercourse expresses and satisfies our need for physical love in the most concrete way possible.

It is my belief that being human means to have the need for love and that the need for love is primary and is then expressed in a physical way in the need for sex. When a human being engages in sexual activity, that individual is attempting to fulfill the need for love—regardless of what the person's sexual preferences or patterns may be. There are, of course, individuals whose particular emotional history and personal makeup hinder them in attaining the state of love. It may be, for instance, that their fear of intimacy makes it difficult for them to open themselves fully to another person, so that in these cases sexuality becomes the only means of obtaining love and thus gives the appearance of being an end in itself. Or, as in a few primitive societies, the expression of love may be at odds with the harsh necessities of mere survival and therefore be prohibited or proscribed. But as we shall see, these exceptions involve a short-circuiting or displacement of the need for love that serves only to accentuate its central importance to being human.

Love, though, particularly reveals its presence in orgasm. No matter how bizarre or even antisocial the circumstances leading up to orgasm may be, the love world is entered at the instant of orgasm. There is always a sense—however momentary—of elevation and extension, of going beyond oneself, of achieving unity with something greater than oneself. What happens to the body during orgasm gives a graphic demonstration of the ultimate nature of the love world.

From day to day, differences in an individual's orgasmic pattern may be caused by such factors as bodily or emotional fatigue, the length of time since orgasm last occurred, or even the temperature of the room. But it is evident that each person has a fairly characteristic set of responses in an active sexual life. These responses are conditioned by the individual's particular ways of being, including standards of behavior and the degree to which the person is able to demonstrate feelings or tries to control them. Yet in spite of all these varying elements, there remain certain overall orgasmic patterns of genital and body response that are basic to all human beings and that show how this peak moment of sexual experience reflects and defines the nature of the love world.

Typically, in reaching an intense orgasm, the entire body becomes rigid. Phenomenologically the person is reaching, extending himself or herself to encompass the totality of existence. The legs and feet are extended, the toes either curled in or flared out in a stiff car-popedal spasm. The shoulders and arms are rigid, grasping, holding. The abdomen becomes hard and spastic. The eyes bulge and stare vacantly or are tightly closed, looking into eternity in either case. The mouth is open as the lungs gasp for additional air, taking in the world in great gulps. Physically we extend ourselves at orgasm to encompass everything. And we feel that we are one with the universe. We no longer stand outside ourselves, reviewing our actions. We have a sense of unity.

Every sexual act is an attempt to achieve that sense of unity. Even to masturbate is to make such an attempt, although the achievement will be limited and transitory. One socially isolated young man who came to me for treatment when in his early twenties had a sexual pattern that consisted of rocking himself in a chair in his locked bedroom while he daydreamed and masturbated compulsively. As a very young child he had been rocked excessively by his parents. A pediatrician advised them that this was unhealthy for the child. But instead of merely cutting down gradually on the amount of rocking, the parents suddenly and totally deprived their young son of this gratifying and security-inducing activity. The child valiantly fought back by consistently rocking himself for a day and a half, until he was exhausted. Yet he was unable to induce his parents to resume the habit. From the child's point of view, to be deprived of the rocking was to be deprived of love. As an adult he was still trying to regain the sense of love by rocking, now accompanied by overt masturbation.

Masturbation is not, of course, necessarily or even usually a neurotic act. During adolescence it can play a significant part in this important developmental phase of human sexuality. For adults, it is a form of pleasurable release that is practiced by a great many men and women as an occasional adjunct to regular sexual intercourse with a loved one. Or it may be used as a substitute for intercourse during periods of separation or when the partner is ill. But it should be understood that masturbation is not merely a matter of physical release; it is a way of entering into the love world, even if only in a solitary, transient manner.

Those who prefer brief transitory sexual encounters with pickups are also seeking a way to enter the love world. I will never forget a patient who was dying of syphilis. In the tertiary stage of syphilis the spirochetes lodge in the aorta, destroying its workings and preventing the proper flow of blood from the heart and diffusion of oxygen through the body. This man's face and body had taken on a swollen, veinous cast, and he gasped for breath. He knew that his increasing cardiovascular failure was caused by the syphilis and was aware that he would probably soon die of his illness. Yet when I discussed his condition with him, he justified the waste of his mature life by smiling and saying, "Ah, the girls, the girls." The girls were prostitutes, and it was from them that he had contracted his disease. Yet for my patient, the encounters with these prostitutes had been precious love experiences, however unilateral or limited.

Unilateral sex will always limit the degree to which the individual enters the love world. For the most essential quality of the love world is its duality. To be in love is to establish a world of two. Significantly, every human being begins life in a world of two. The child in the mother's womb gives the pregnant woman the emotional strength of two. Suicides among pregnant women are extremely rare exactly because of the mother's awareness that her world is a dual one. In the womb the child draws its strength and its sense of security from the fact that it too inhabits a world of two. Once the child is born, it must continue to have a sense of being loved; as we have seen, if the child cannot derive that sense from being touched and held, it cannot develop in a healthy way.

As adults we seek love not just to satisfy our sexual needs but to establish emotional and physical unity with another human being. It is no accident that the creation myths in so many of the world's cultures involve the splitting of one into two. Plato's concept that we constantly seek to reunite ourselves with the "lost" half of our being can be viewed, for instance, in a phenomenological way. It is as though we carried about with ourselves, as a part of our body image, a sense of what is necessary to make us complete, to make us one. The joining of penis and vagina creates a physical unity. At orgasm, the sense of a transcending unity will emerge into momentary existence even for casual partners who will never see one another again. But for two people who love one another, there is an added dimension, a perduring sense of enlargement. For loving couples, the love world does not end with orgasm; it is not completed by sexual satisfaction but rather extended by it.

Two individuals joined together in the love world not only have their own personal experience, perceptions, imagination and intelligence to draw on, but also partake of the partner's perceptions, experiences, and intelligence. Thus there is an increase in the magnitude of one's existence that fosters a new view of being and of the world. Automatically one is strengthened, and the twoness that is created is no mere summation of the two individuals but a multiplication of the sense of life's possibilities for both of them.

The duality of the love world changes our perception of both time and space. During a sexual experience we switch over from standard clock time to what might be called experiential time. We are in "another world," and we lose track of the passage of time in our ordinary daily world. At the moment of orgasm time—for an instant—seems unending. This is true no matter how orgasm is achieved, even through masturbation. After orgasm, as we return to the ordinary world, it is often necessary to check to see what the clock time is. We may be surprised to see that *only* ten minutes have passed; we have, after all, been in a world in which we have experienced a sense of eternity. We may be equally astonished to discover that an entire hour has passed in what seemed "no time at all." For the period of their lovemaking, partners exist beyond time. This alteration of the sense of time occurs only during the sex act itself for the person who achieves orgasm through masturbation or with a temporary partner. But for partners immersed in a love relationship, the sense of time continues to be altered in the mundane daily world as well.

Once a person enters extensively into the love world—that is, begins to exist as a lover—the duality of that world, its twoness, is always present in the life of the individual, even if the partner is physically absent. In the love world all things are seen as having a future. This "looking forward" is physically manifested in the eyes. Whether one is in love or not, the pupils of the eyes become dilated at orgasm, as though looking beyond the moment into eternity. For lovers, however, the dilation of the pupils does not occur only at orgasm; it has been found to carry over into ordinary daily life as well. Couples who love one another have a lot more eye contact in general than nonlovers, "drinking" one another in and at the same time seeing beyond the self. Thus lovers exist in the three dimensions of time, simultaneously encompassing their past together, their present together, and the future they look to together.

The sense of infinity that we experience at orgasm, of being at one with the basic pulse of the universe, continues to be felt to some extent in the ordinary world by lovers. That is why it seems so romantic, for example, for lovers to stand on a beach at night, watching the endless roll of the ocean beneath the stars. The poetry of love throughout the ages has made use of imagery involving the ocean, the heavens, and the infinite exactly because of the sense of enduring amplitude that we experience in the love world. The suicides and love deaths that occur in the stories of Romeo and Juliet, Tristan and Isolde, and the Mayerling tragedy are accepted by these mythic and literary characters with a kind of equanimity because they feel themselves to be living in an infinite universe in which they will always be together.

The sense of space is also changed in the love world. Between lovers there is no great sense of distance—everything is in reach. Two lovers who find themselves physically separated by a continent are still closer together than two strangers squeezed up against one another in a subway car at rush hour. In the love world, as in the Einsteinian universe, space is curved; there are no sharp, rough edges that might induce a sundering. This sense of infinitude, however, is experienced in a very personal way; the universe seems to belong to the lovers alone, extensive but also private. The exclusivity of the love world is evident in the special feeling that a woman experienced when she was walking along a crowded street with her lover, a feeling of being enclosed in a large shining bubble as they moved together through the throngs. Without the presence of her lover, she said, she was always aware of people pushing and bumping as they hurried along, breaking into the world she was trying to occupy. But with her lover she always had the sense of that giant bubble's enclosing and protecting them.

When two partners fall out of love, that bubble bursts. It is a wrenching experience that is felt not only emotionally but physically. The light(ness) has gone out of the world, and a cardinal symptom of the depression that follows the loss of a loved one is the feeling of a ball in the chest, a leaden weight at the emotional center of our being, the heart area. That weight can be so heavy that one feels one is falling—

out of the love world. People who have lost a lover tend to carry themselves with a certain tightness, as though trying to hold themselves together in a bodily way, to prevent themselves from falling. The head is held more stiffly; movement is slowed and is more rigid. Even in sleep the bereaved lover will demonstrate the feeling of loss, moving restlessly in an attempt to contact the missing partner, flailing in empty space, or drawing the body in upon itself, seeking security in the sheltering corners of the bed.

The changes in our perception of time and space in the love world depend on the duality of the lovers' relationship; it is a world created by two. If those two people fall out of love, the love world will cease to exist for them in its full dimensions until they are able to form new relationships and create a new duality. Yet whatever sexual activity a person engages in, even when not in love, will be an attempt to enter once more into the love world, even if only in a temporary way.

In recent years, of course, there has been a tendency to sound the death knell of romantic love and even to question its very existence. Symposia on love were held at the American Psychological Association conventions in both 1970 and 1971, and some social behaviorists among the panel members cast an extremely cold eye on the concept of love. According to one argument put forward, love "may be viewed as a consequence of the needs for self-esteem, sexual satisfaction, and conformity to social pressures." All three elements were seen as combining to make love "necessary." The individual who boosts our ego by liking us and liking the same things we do, and who has sex appeal as well, elicits our "love." To have sex without love in our society induces guilt, with an accompanying frustration and anxiety, because it is not socially approved. But if we say that we "love" the person who boosts our ego and gives us sexual satisfaction and we marry that person, our satisfaction is given the stamp of approval.

Another panelist took an economic point of view, beginning with the premise that for a person to use hard-earned money to support other people was basically "irrational." However, the economic structure of our society demands that people get married and have children in order to provide a sufficient consumer base. If sex without love were permitted, there would be no need for marriage and family, and the consumer base would be destroyed. Thus love, in this view, becomes a societal invention necessary to persuade people to create successive nuclear family consumer units.

Other social behaviorists have gone even further, equating love with fear. According to this viewpoint, if an individual finds deep satisfaction in a relationship, there would inevitably be an increase in fear; the dependency of the "love" relationship would bring with it a correlative fear of losing the person providing their gratification. Thus love has been defined as "the fear of losing an important source of need gratification." Under such a definition the romantic cry "I can't live without you" is seen as an expression of extreme panic.

Paralleling the current trend toward explaining love in terms of social pressures, economics, or fear, there has been an increased emphasis on purely genital sex. Kierkegaard's phrase "To see her is to love her" might more likely be expressed today as "To see her is to want her." Stendhal, writing of love at first sight, spoke of the sudden sensation of recognition and hope that arose in the lover. Today it is more likely to be "lust at first sight," with the sensation of recognition and hope being translated into "Maybe that's someone I can make it with." Yet a great many people find that the emphasis on purely genital sex leaves them feeling empty and alone. In her recent study of sexual patterns, based on interviews, Rosemarie Santini found that a recurring theme among those interviewed was a sense that the problem in today's society was not in finding a sexual partner but rather in feeling something in the course of the sexual experience.

It is true that the divorce rate is climbing ever higher in our society. It is true that the "trial marriages" of some couples—though certainly not all—seem to be based on the same sort of motivation as ordering a set of cookware on thirty-day approval. But while we may be changing partners more often and altering our approach to the choosing of our partners in some ways, it cannot be maintained that people are any less in need of love. Couples do not, after all, get married with the *expectation* of getting divorced. The majority of young people who live together without getting married would say that they are in love. But there is no longer a traditional dating-engagement-marriage pattern to go by. It is no longer a "big thing" to live together without getting married. And having seen the marriages of parents, relatives, and friends break up, many people do not want to formalize matters too quickly when it is unnecessary to do so. Nevertheless, people do seek out partners not just to have sex with but to live with and to love.

Because it is so much easier to get divorced than it used to be—as well as much more socially acceptable—married couples who no longer love one another now separate in cases where they might formerly have stayed together, unloving, because of social pressures. It is highly significant that the great majority of divorced individuals soon remarry. Why should they do so in a world in which it is so easy to have sex without commitment, genital variety without personal intimacy? The answer is obvious. They want to enter the love world, and sex is not an end in itself but rather a means for experiencing the special enlargement and extension of our beings that occur in the love world. It is worth considering, indeed, that the rising divorce rates may indicate an increase in the number of people demanding their right to love and be loved, people willing to put their need for love above such previously more powerful forces as security, social convention, and family cohesion. We live in a society that has become depersonalized in so many ways that the need for love, rather than diminishing, seems likely to become more urgent. The difficulty is that our society has in recent years put so much emphasis on sex as a technique that many people have lost sight of its connections with personality and with love. It is my hope that this book will help individuals to understand better those connections, for within the love world, sex, personality, and love coincide, become parts of a whole rather than separate and even contradictory elements.

Sex does not take place in a vacuum. Our sexual lives reflect our personal lives, both the individual essence of ourselves *and* the effects that the culture that nurtured us have had upon our particular shaping as human beings. The more sophisticated the society, the greater the range of personal choice is likely to be, the greater the differences between individuals. In a primitive society, of course, where personal choice must give way before the sheer matter of survival, sexual taboos and strictures are at their most intense. But it is important to remember that sexual practices must always be viewed within the context of the society as a whole. Studying the Manus of New Guinea, Margaret Mead found that the women regarded sex as both shameful and painful and that all their affection was focused on their children. Sexual intercourse with their husbands was regarded as a kind of humiliation, and since the society had strong taboos against any kind of foreplay, intercourse became almost a kind of rape.

But this does not mean that the need for love did not exist among the Manus; it means simply that within the context of their society it was impossible to give open *expression* to that need. The Manus lived in a precarious and uncertain world. As a matter of survival, they could not afford to allow the spontaneity and idealism of love to exist because it would add still another element of uncertainty to their world. As in all cultures, the Manus recognized the necessity for sexual activity; like all societies, they practiced a form of marriage. But their marriages were completely utilitarian, disconnected from love.

Utilitarian marriages are common in certain advanced societies as well, but the greater scope of a highly developed civilization allows for the expression of love in other ways. The French culture is a case in point. French children are trained to be productive and conservative and to trust only the family unit. They are taught that the enjoyment of adult pleasures—food and sex—depends on acquiring the kind of job and status that will provide the money necessary for the pursuit of these pleasures. Marriage is seen not as romantic but as planned and rational, an adjunct of status. Thus there is great tolerance for sexual affairs outside the marriage. *L'amour* is not what one feels for one's marriage partner; rather, it is the term for a sexual game, in which much of the pleasure is derived from the pursuit. For the French, love is connected with spontaneity, pleasure, and physicality. In the marriage relationship these elements are downplayed, while intimacy and commitment are accentuated.

In the United States the individual expects the marriage partner to be lover as well as husband or wife. When this dual role is achieved, the elements of intimacy, spontaneity, pleasure, physicality, and commitment all are brought together into single focus. The French, who have an extreme realism concerning human emotions, would undoubtedly claim that this dual role and fusion of elements are more than can be reasonably anticipated from a single relationship and so choose to separate marriage from love.

Cultural heritage does not merely affect conceptions of marriage and their relationship to love, however; specific sexual practices are also emphasized or forbidden according to overall societal rules. This fact is of particular interest in the light of the current fascination with Oriental sexual techniques in Western countries, America in particular. A number of recent books and articles, for instance, have made a great deal of the Indian, Japanese, and Chinese techniques by which the male prevents himself from ejaculating and is thus able to maintain an erection for extraordinary lengths of time. These techniques may make it possible for a woman to enjoy her potential for multiple orgasms and at the same time give some men a gratifying sense of their own virility. But any Western couple experimenting with them should be aware of the specific cultural reasons for their development in Eastern societies.

In India, for example, it was believed for centuries—and among some sects is still believed—that semen emanated from a man's brain and that each ejaculation involved a spending of the man's vital force. Thus, by avoiding ejaculation, the man's aim was not so much to increase his wife's pleasure as it was to preserve his own life-force. In China the retention of semen was connected with the spiritual concept of yang and yin, the male and female forces believed to be present in all things, complementary, yet inseparable. It was believed that sexual intercourse stimulated the yang in men and the yin in women, but that if orgasm occurred, the vital forces would be absorbed by the partner.

Thus, in ancient China, a paternalistic culture, the object of frequent or continuous intercourse without orgasm was to allow the man to absorb as much of the vital force of the woman as possible into his own being. For the elderly, it was regarded as wise to have intercourse with women who were young and vigorous since they had more vital force to give. Some women, whose station allowed them the luxury of many sexual consorts, turned the tables on the men, attempting to increase their longevity by having frequent intercourse with young boys, drawing from them their youthful and life-sustaining semen. There are many stories of this nature about the mythical Chinese queen mother of the West, Hsi Wang Mu, who was said to retain her beauty and immortality by this means.

Since Chinese society was polygamous, there was another aspect to the retention of semen. Any man of means was expected to have several wives, and by avoiding ejaculation, he was able to have intercourse with each of them more often. In addition, it was believed that by absorbing the vital force from these wives without having an orgasm, he would be especially potent when he did allow himself to ejaculate with the wife chosen to bear his latest child and thus might expect that fertilization would take place and that the child would be a strong one.

Therefore, we can see that the avoidance of ejaculation, which is currently being presented to Western readers simply as a sexual technique, is something much more than that. The retention of semen in the Orient is connected to a whole way of life, a view of the world that has its particular personal, societal, and even religious aspects. A Western man who attempts this technique and finds it difficult to master certainly should not feel any sense of failure. For he does not have either the world view or the cultural pressures that made its mastery significant and important in the Orient.

No sexual act, indeed, is merely a matter of technique. In this book I shall relate the specific sexual acts in which people engage to the feeling they have about themselves as unique human beings. All sexual activities—the positions, patterns, and habits—through which we express ourselves reflect the whole person. I hope that the reader, by examining the concrete texture of sexual activity and sensation from a phenome-nological point of view and by seeing that our sexual activities exist within the larger context of the love world, will be stimulated to look at his or her own ex-perience of the love world in a new way.

One loves the way one lives. We enter into sexual intimacy with another human being with characteris-tic ways of behaving: defending ourselves where we feel vulnerable but at the same time testing and ex-ploring the possibilities of relationship with another. Some individuals, of course, find it necessary to con-centrate more on defending themselves against anxiety than they do exploring the duality that can be cre-ated with the loved one. It is the great paradox of the love world that the strongest individuals, those whose sense of themselves is most highly developed, are most able to let go, can most freely abandon themselves to the love world. The very strength of their personality gives them the assurance that they can bounce back, can reassert their individuality, and thus they do not hesitate to surrender themselves to the duality of the love relationship.

During sexual intimacy we live predominantly as we always do, using our individual and characteristic modes of dealing with situations. Yet because love en-courages us to hold ourselves open to a new world of sensation and relationship that is at every moment a creation and an adventure, we have the opportunity in the love world to transcend our own limitations in a way that few other human activities offer. The public today is presented with a confusion of "how-to" ap-proaches to sexuality, some emphasizing instrumental-ized pleasure seeking, others pure hedonism, and some a manipulation that involves control, detachment, and power in human relationships. I believe that by learn-ing to look at their sexual choices in terms of their overall ways of being rather than in terms of mere technique, individuals will be better able to under-stand and deal with their own and their partners' sexuality. And I feel certain that by recognizing that each individual makes use of his or her sexuality in order to find a pathway into the love world, those individuals can discover fresh meaning and importance in the sexual act itself.

CHAPTER 3

The Sexual Stage

As with any drama, the stage setting in which the act
of love is carried out can enhance or detract from the
emotional intensity of the experience. But in this case
the setting is of consequence only to the actors; there
is usually no audience. Those situations in which an
audience is present are in one way or another highly
ritualistic ones. In twelfth-century Cambodia, for instance, it was the custom for brides to be sexually initiated by a priest in the presence of the wedding
guests. The priests were paid handsomely for their
services, with those noted for their expertise drawing
the highest rewards. No priest was allowed to
perform this ceremony more than once a year and
was presumed to remain celibate otherwise. From the
psychoanalytic point of view, such customs are seen
as a way of ensuring that any pain the bride may experience during sexual initiation will not be held
against the groom who has been chosen for her by her
parents; any negative feelings the bride may have are
given a ritual outlet.

More recently, in eighteenth-century England, the
wedding guests sometimes attended the sexual initiation of the newly married couple, although the
groom himself performed the act. The bridesmaids
would lead the bride to the nuptial chamber, undress
her, and place her on the bed. The groom was
undressed by his male friends in another room and
then brought into the bedroom. The couple then had

intercourse while their guests clustered around the
bed, offering ribald encouragement.

Obviously, in order to perform under such public
scrutiny, the wedding couple could have had few
qualms concerning either their physicality or the enjoyment of sensory pleasure. But other qualities of the
love world, particularly intimacy and spontaneity,
would necessarily be sacrificed. Indeed, privacy during the sexual act is basic to the full achievement of
the love world. Only in a very few isolated cultures is
sexual intercourse carried out regularly in the presence
of others. In both the examples mentioned above, the
public performance took place only once and under
ritualized circumstances.

Even among primitive societies, privacy is generally
sought out by the couple. In the classic work *Patterns
of Sexual Behavior*, by Clellan S. Ford and Frank A.
Beach, a study shows that people living "in unpartitioned, multiple dwellings rather than private family
dwellings prefer to have sexual relations outdoors by a
ratio of 9 to 1." The Kiwai tribe demonstrates the
desire for privacy particularly clearly, since its dwellings have changed form over the years. When they
formerly lived in long, unpartitioned houses sheltering
several families, the Kiwai usually had intercourse in
the privacy of the bush, making use of the natural
screening of the surrounding vegetation. But today,
living in small one-family houses, these people have
changed their customary pattern, and marital intercourse takes place in a separate room in the house.

The importance of privacy in the sexual environment is not just a matter of courtesy or inhibition,
however. For if the qualities of timelessness and of a
foreshortened spatial intimacy that characterize the
love world are to be achieved, privacy is essential.
One reason alleged for the popularity of group sex
among some couples in recent years is that it sup-
posedly allows the couple to explore the purely genital aspects of sex without arousing fears that one's

husband or wife may experience anything beyond
sexual arousal and release. The lack of privacy in
group sex precludes any extensive entry into the love
world. Some couples even make the claim that group
sex is relatively unthreatening to the marriage relationship because of the lack of emotional involvement.

Privacy carries with it, of course, a sense of security. The sexual act may take time. If, for fear of
interruption, it must be hurried, full entrance into the
love world will be difficult to achieve. The qualities of
timelessness, transcendence, and fusion that are the ultimate objective of the sex-love relationship constitute
a fragile emotional web. Ringing telephones, children
playing in the next room, a playful cat or dog that de-
cides to get in on the act—any and all reminders of the
activities and responsibilities of our daily existence can
easily disrupt the strands of that web. The couple
who go off for a week to the Bahamas or the moun-
tains on a "second honeymoon," separating themselves
briefly from jobs, children and neighbors, are specifically trying to re-create a private world in which
they need have concern only for one another. It is the
sense of privacy that makes such a trip "romantic."

Yet exactly because the security of privacy is so essential to the love world, there can be for some couples a special excitement and a heightened sense of
fusion if they are able to transcend the daily world
even while it is close at hand. One young couple at
the beginning of a passionate relationship were spending a few days on a Caribbean resort island. As they
explored one another physically and emotionally, they
experimented with a number of different love making
situations. The young woman suggested, in response
to a fantasy of hers, that they make love near an open
window in the living room. The window was in clear
view of a walkway a few feet from the house, along
which people were constantly passing. For the woman,
the charm of the situation was that they would
be able to enter into their private love existence

even while being able to see the world passing by a
few feet away. For both of them, however, the intrusion of the outside world proved too disturbing,
and they were unable to sustain the fantasy. The risk
of being seen was apparently too great, and they had
to abandon the situation and begin again in another
room. Thus, while the idea of flouting the conventions of privacy and undercutting the security it
brings may be exciting in the abstract, many people
find that they cannot do so in actuality.

To make love in natural surroundings—in the woods
or a meadow, on a beach, or in the sea itself—has always had strong romantic appeal. The love scene between Deborah Kerr and Burt Lancaster at the water's
edge in *From Here to Eternity*, which was considered
profoundly erotic when the film was made in 1953,
retains much of its power in our own much franker
day exactly because of the natural environment in
which it occurs. But it should be noted that the two
characters in that scene were absolutely alone on the
beach. Sexual intercourse in natural surroundings is
regarded as romantic only when the element of privacy is present; indeed, to be "away from it all" in a
great open space actually increases the sense of privacy even though one is outdoors.

Sex in a natural setting involves another important
aspect of environmental impact on the love world: the
simple matter of comfort. In terms of actual sex positions, as we shall see in later chapters, comfort often
gives way to the excitement of the moment; muscular
strain on the legs, arms, or back can be totally ignored
during intercourse. But environmental discomfort is a
different matter. Flies or mosquitoes, extreme heat or
cold, loud noises, or flashing lights act as an irritant,
reminding the couple of the ordinary world around
them and making it difficult to enter fully into the
love world. There is an amusing sequence in the original *Pink Panther* film in which a couple make love in
a sled amid the snows of a Swiss mountain resort. The

man obviously fails, and to the petulant complaint of his female partner, he replies, "What do you expect at twenty degrees below zero in a sled in the snow?" Love may keep us warm, but not under those conditions.

Temperature is a key environmental aspect of the sex act. Throughout history, in all cultures and languages, the sun's heat and the body's warmth—or lack of it—have been at the heart of sexual metaphor. From the "warm flush" that Dante felt upon his first sight of Beatrice to a contemporary slang phrase like "hot to trot," sex has been associated with an elevation of temperature. "Hot and moist" immediately indicates sexuality, "dry and cold" a rejection of it. Pornographic literature down through the ages abounds with images of heat in reference to both the male and the female organs. A considerable degree of male chauvinism shows itself in such sexual imagery, however. The language of heat is most often used in respect to the female, while words of weaponry and power, such as "lance" or "sword," are attached to the male. This was carried through into technical terms: A woman with sexual difficulties was frigid, while a man was impotent.

One patient of mine told of going to a prostitute who obviously had a thorough understanding of the importance of temperature to sex. Before performing fellatio on the man, she rinsed her mouth with hot water. He found the sensation extremely exciting and told her so. She replied that the next time he came to see her she would put ice cubes in her mouth beforehand and assured him he would find that even more stimulating.

During intercourse, heat and cold can have a striking effect upon both the sensory and the psychological ways in which we experience sex. The skin is one of our major sensory organs, especially adapted to the perception of temperature. If a person has spent the day at the beach in the sun, the pores of the skin will be open and enlarged. The touch of the partner's hand or lips on the skin will then be felt with particular sensitivity, even to the point of pain if the skin is sunburned. But on a cool day, when the pores are closed, the skin will be especially soft and smooth, affording an entirely different kind of sensory experience. When the pores are open and the skin is especially sensitive, the physical aspects of intercourse are likely to be heightened, but often to a degree that is distracting since both partners will be unusually aware of their own particular body responses. When the pores are closed on a cool day and the skin is less sensitive but smoother, a greater pleasure in the body of the partner is likely to be experienced, making it possible to achieve a more profound sense of fusion.

Extremes of temperature can heighten the sexual experience. To make love in front of a roaring fire, to snuggle under a down quilt on a sub-zero night, or to slither about in the sweat of one another's bodies on a tropical night can sometimes make intercourse particularly exciting. But often in such cases the pleasure is primarily psychological. In front of the fire, one's feet may be freezing cold and one's shoulders burning hot. In purely physical terms one is uncomfortable; the pleasure is derived from the sense of being safe and alone with one's partner while the wind howls outside.

An unpleasant physical environment can have long-term effects on a couple's sexual relationship. One young woman went to London to join her lover, a man she had met in Europe some months before. They had been separated for six weeks and could not wait to be together again. But because of money problems, they were forced to take a dingy, damp, and chilly basement apartment. During the month that they lived there, they had intercourse only a few times in spite of the fact that they continued to have an intense love relationship. According to the young woman, the cold dampness of their surroundings was so at odds with the way they felt about one another that it seemed to rob them of sexual desire. It was not until they moved into a new light and warm apartment that their physical passion for one another reasserted itself. "It was very strange," the young woman said. "I've always enjoyed sex a lot, and I was wild about Jerry, but there was something about that miserable basement that made sex seem beside the point, almost dirty."

For this young woman, it seems clear that the general grubbiness of the furnished flat she and her lover shared had as much to do with turning her off sexually as did the dampness and cold. For most people, the colors, furniture, and fabrics used in a bedroom are extremely important. We should not forget that the entire environment in which one chooses to live reflects the individuality of the person. And the bedroom is often the room in which that individuality is most clearly evident. In design magazines that feature the homes of actual people, as well as the owners' comments on their decorative choices, the importance of the bedroom is often emphasized. Many people point out that while the living room and dining room are places in which they entertain guests and are therefore designed to some extent with other people's comfort and even taste in mind, the bedroom remains an intensely personal domain. The owner will say, "This room was designed for me."

It is interesting to note that in bachelor establishments, the bedrooms are often very different from those in the homes of married couples. The male bedrooms tend to make use of dark colors, browns, maroons, and other earth tones; the furnishings are apt to be simple and dramatic. The bedrooms of couples, on the other hand, are often somewhat frilly and make use of pastel colors. In many cases the husband will admit—or even declare somewhat defensively—that the decoration of the bedroom was entirely up to his wife. Left to his own devices, then, the male appears to prefer to make his bedroom into something of a lair, dark and sensual. Yet upon marrying, he allows his wife to decorate the bedroom according to her taste.

Even post-women's-liberation studies of sexuality show that in most cases sexual arousal in men is initially a very physical matter, while in women it tends to be more emotional. In terms of the environment this difference between the sexes shows itself particularly in respect to the favored sexual environment of the teenage male, the automobile. To some extent cars are used by young men for sex simply because that is the only place available. But even when other alternatives may exist, many young men actively enjoy having sex in their cars. The car is one of the first expressions of freedom and power that the young male has access to. But while sex in a car is exciting to many males, it is often disturbing to women. Even if a young woman is perfectly willing to have intercourse with her boyfriend under other circumstances, she may well resist his motorized advances. For many women, the cramped back seat of a car is an environment that is inimical to emotional arousal; indeed, far from being titillating, such surroundings may seem comical.

The center of the sexual environment is, of course, the bed. But different kinds of beds can create widely divergent kinds of environments. At one extreme there are the king-size or huge round beds covered with furs and surrounded by mirrors that some sports and rock stars appear to take such pleasure in displaying to the world in newspaper and magazine stories. Such beds resemble miniature stages, complete with dramatic lighting, and seem entirely appropriate for these young men who are constantly in the limelight—even when in bed—and who appear to have a different girlfriend every week.

Several specialized sexual environments have become popular in recent years. Water beds, according to those who use them, provide not only a sense of undulating buoyancy but also a rhythmic sensuosity that makes the environment seem in tune with the couple as they make love. Loft beds are increasingly seen in small city apartments. They are space savers, but more interestingly they create a private environment that is elevated above the plane of daily existence. The same effect is achieved on a more elaborate scale with sleep boxes, costing thousands of dollars; these custom-made environments are virtual rooms in themselves and can be tailored to the most exotic tastes. It is obvious that any couple buying such a bed puts a very high premium on having a personalized sexual environment.

Most of us, though, sleep and make love on a plain store-bought box spring and mattress. Its hardness or softness is determined more by our sleeping comfort than by any sexual consideration. Yet even with the plainest of beds we attempt to make this utilitarian environment our own, giving it personality and individuality by our choice of sheets, blankets, and quilts. We develop proprietary feelings about our beds; we do not like to have other people sleep in them and certainly not to make love in them. To the majority of people, the idea of buying a secondhand mattress is abhorrent, even though it has been re-covered and is far "cleaner" than the one we have been using for several years. A chair is a chair, and we are delighted to acquire an old rocker at a country auction. But our beds are extremely personal. The uneasy night or two of sleep we pass in a strange bed has little to do with its physical characteristics. It is the fact that this different bed is an alien *environment* that bothers us; usually we feel no such restlessness sleeping on a brand-new mattress that we have bought and know is *ours*. Our own bed is a secure environment in which we feel no qualms about letting ourselves go, whether to relax into the sleep world or to abandon ourselves to the love world.

Our beds are not only the stage upon which we act
out our adult passions but also the rehearsal hall in
which adolescents experiment with and learn about
their bodies. Usually this learning process is a solitary
and masturbatory one, but in a number of past societies the bed was also a place of courtship. During the
nineteenth century the tradition of bundling was common in New England, in Wales, and in the Hebrides
Islands off the coast of Scotland. Young spooning
couples were allowed to use the family bedroom to
carry on their courtship in private. During cold
weather the only fire in the cottage or farmhouse
would be in the living room or kitchen. Fuel, then as
now, was in short supply, and the entire family would
gather in the one room with a fire. The lack of privacy in such a situation made it difficult for young
couples to form the kind of intimate relationship that
would lead to marriage. To give the courting couple a
chance to be alone, while still providing them with
warmth, they were allowed to lie beneath the covers
in the bedroom, snug and comfortable, but prevented
from having actual intercourse by one of two methods: Either a wooden board was placed down the
center of the bed or the maiden's thighs were bound
together with a special knot. No doubt some young
couples managed to circumvent the precautions of the
knot or of bed and board, but it seems likely that the
environment of the bundling bed set up psychological
barriers to intercourse that were more effective than
the actual physical restraints.

We have seen that the environment in which we attempt to enter the love world can enhance or restrict
our ability to let ourselves go. Our surroundings can
affect us during all phases of the sexual cycle. But
even when the surroundings are conducive to sex, the
couple must create between them at the outset a psychological climate that will make it possible for mutual arousal to take place. There are various signs and

signals that couples use to indicate to one another that
sex is desired. These announcements of intention can
take a great many forms, with the particular form employed reflecting the overall relationship between the
couple. Like the overture at the beginning of a musical or opera, these initiatory procedures not only indicate that the curtain is about to rise but also give a
forecast of the kind of drama that is to ensue.

For instance, one highly obsessive young man, who
saw sex as something sinful and dirty, would take a
pair of his wife's stockings and throw them on the
bed in order to say, "Prepare for sex." Since he was
unable to initiate sex in a tender or romantic way, he
threw down the stockings like a gauntlet; only by is-
suing a kind of challenge could he overcome his own
negative feelings about sex. What was more, this man
was something of a fetishist and insisted that his wife
wear black silk stockings during coitus. Thus his overtures were in tune with the sex experience to follow.

In another case a wife would become very aggressive and provocative toward her husband, causing
an argument. The conflict would then be laid to rest
in an annealing sexual embrace. The initiation of sex
through the device of picking a fight has an obvious
sadomasochistic overlay and often demonstrates difficulties in open communication between the partners
in their whole relationship. The couple mentioned
here eventually divorced, but there are other partners
for whom this pattern of quarreling and "making up"
is not only satisfying but the only way in which the
love world can be entered.

The desire for sex is not always indicated in such
dramatic ways, however. Subtle body signals or
changes in vocal patterns may be used. Increased eye
contact, affectionate touching of the partner, especially in erogeneous areas, or a languorousness and
huskiness of the voice all may be employed to an-
nounce to the partner a need to enter the love world.
The individual's movements may become more rhyth-

mic, anticipating the sexual act in a bodily way. Some
people, on the other hand, show signs of tension, the
body held stiffly in check, as though preparing to leap
forward. The voice may become more intense, even
shrill, especially in individuals who tend to be very
vocal during intercourse.

The variety of signals used can range from the
mildly flirtatious to the grossly exhibitionistic, from
coquettishly fluttered eyelids, a lightly lascivious lick-
ing of the lips, to a blatant unzipping or removal of
clothing. But in each case the signals used will be expressive of the characteristic way of living in the
world that is intrinsic to the person employing them,
establishing from the beginning the thematic unity of
the individual's way of behaving. But at the same time
the overtures made will be consistent with not only
the psychological but the environmental situation in
which they are taking place. Thus a couple who when
at home might actively squeeze or caress the partner
in an overtly erogenous area will instead touch knees
under the table in a restaurant. .

The situational aspects of such signals can cause
confusion between couples. For instance, one of my
patients, a married woman, was having an affair with a
married man. Their meetings had to be secretly ar-
ranged, and it was not always possible for them to
do more than have lunch together. When they did
make love, it would be in a rented hotel room. Whenever they met, the woman would ask, "Are we going
to a hotel?" This was a way of establishing the agenda
for the day; the woman needed to know how long
they were going to be together so that she could
prepare an explanation for her activities during that
period of time. But the man took it for more than this,
regarding the question as an indication of her passionate interest in him. Later, when this couple had
actually been living together for a time, the woman
wanted to return to what she felt to be a more natural
kind of interaction and would wait for him to suggest

that they make love. However, the man mistakenly assumed that this change in signals meant a diminishment of her romantic feelings for him.

In another case a verbal sign of this sort became a code word understood by both partners. This couple usually had intercourse only on weekends. The husband was a extremely timorous man and found it difficult to speak directly about sex. Thus, when he wanted to make love at unexpected times, he would ask his wife for a "weekend." In this relationship, because of the man's reticence, sex was not an ordinary assumed matter but a "special occasion." Only by placing his desires in this framework was the man able to muster the assertiveness to make overtures to his wife.

The sexual stage is set. Whether the love encounter takes place on a beach at night during a weekend by the sea or in the context of a Tuesday night "weekend" in a city apartment, the physical environment affects the nature of the act. The climate of feeling between the partners may be altered by the setting, and in such cases the code that exists between the partners to indicate a desire to enter into the love world may also undergo changes.

But whatever the setting and whatever form the overture to sexual arousal may take, it should be remembered that each of us is also an environment in ourselves. Our bodies have form, texture, odor. In the act of making love we not only see, hear, and touch our partners but taste and smell them as well. It is this realm of the senses that we will be exploring in the next chapter as the central drama begins to unfold.

CHAPTER 4

Sex and the Senses

Of the five commonly known senses—sight, smell, hearing, taste, and touch—the most important to the sex-love experience is touch. As mentioned in Chapter One, the human infant requires a large amount of touching in order for healthy development to take place; a lack of touching can in severe instances even cause the infant to die. Among animals and in many primitive human societies the grooming of other members of the group determines the ability to relate in an interpersonal way. Because of the importance of touch to our development, it is the sense that is most strongly associated with security and with feelings of tenderness. In the case of Helen Keller, for example, the sense of touch provided the only entrance through which she could arrive at an eventual understanding of the physiognomy of a world she could neither see nor hear.

The organ of touch in the human is primarily the skin. The skin contains areas of special sexual sensitivity that constitute the so-called erogenous zones. Aside from the genitals themselves, the lips and tongue are most profoundly involved in the touch-oriented aspects of sex. However, any portion of the skin may become an erogenous zone because of early stimulation patterns, natural sensitivity, or learned behavior. There is an interesting case of a young woman with three lovers, each of whom travels extensively, so that the young woman spends only a few days with

each man every few weeks. She claims that her erogenous zones change according to which man she is
with, as though adapting to each one's particular ways
of making love.

The peoples of different cultures show differing
degrees of tolerance or desire for touching. The
Japanese are extremely touch-positive. Southern Europeans and Latin Americans exhibit strong touch behavior. The English and Scandinavians are far more
reserved about touching one another. Until recently
Americans have shied away from open touching.
Many American men, in particular, have in the past
been reluctant to touch people in an affectionate,
casual way. The man would embrace his wife or children in a somewhat formal manner or shake a male
friend's hand, but he would seldom reach out to
stroke, pat, or fondle even the members of his own
family. From the late nineteenth century well into the
twentieth century, such behavior was considered un-
manly. There appears to have been a strong feeling
that touching was indicative of sexual feeling, and
therefore, it was ruled out except in the privacy of
the marriage bed.

One fascinating study reveals that couples sitting together in Paris or Puerto Rico touch each other on
the average of 100 to 200 times an hour. During the
same period an American couple might exchange a pat
or two, while a typical British couple would not
touch at all during an hour's conversation. In the past
twenty years a great deal has changed in the United
States and elsewhere in respect to touching. On the
part of both sexes, open affectionate touching has become increasingly prevalent among the younger age
group. It is interesting that this increase in touching
has coincided with the so-called sexual revolution
since as a general rule the more touching a person is
capable of, the more likely he or she is to be open to
sexual and love experiences.

It has been shown that clothed infants are less active

than unclothed babies. Clothing apparently reduces the ability for skin stimulation and therefore inhibits activity in general. In puritanical societies it is common for some form of clothing to be worn even during sexual intercourse. Many Victorian couples never saw one another naked in the course of decades of marriage. But the connection between clothing and sexual inhibition is not merely psychological. Clothing prevents skin from touching skin and thus deprives the couple of the use of one of the major organs of sexual gratification.

Certain areas of the body are more touch-sensitive sexually than others. Aside from the genital area itself, the most sensitive areas for both men and women are the nipples, the navel, the armpits, inside the upper thighs, and, posteriorly, the nape of the neck, the length of the spine, and the buttocks. Men are generally more sensitive in the area of the ear than women, while the sensitivity of the throat is greater in women than men. Women are, in addition, especially stimulated by a touch at the back of the knees. The majority of women readily respond to the stimulation of the nipples, but there are a surprising number who attest that they find it irritating and even painful to have their nipples fondled or sucked. Both men and women have one or two body areas that are particularly sensitive, and these areas may vary considerably from person to person.

In terms of the genital organs, there is a hierarchy of sensitivity determined by nerve distribution in the genital area. The clitoris is the most sensitive area for women, followed by the rim of the vagina, the inner lips (labia minora), and the outer lips (labia majora). Some women are more stimulated on one side of the genital lips than the other. The most sensitive area of the male genitals is the frenulum—on the underside of the penis where the glans meets the shaft—followed by the tip of the penis, the rim of the glans, the shaft, and, finally, the testicles. The diamond-shaped area that lies between the genitals and the anus, called the perineal region, is sensitive for both men and women, but especially for women. And both sexes are highly sensitive in the perianal area.

In discussing the genitals, many of my female patients have referred to the feel of the penis in the hand. The fact that the penis is so soft when flaccid and bone hard when erect provides a striking perceptual experience for women. They describe the touch of the skin of the penis as smooth, velvety, or soft as silk and are struck by how different it feels from the way it looks.

During a study I conducted in the 1950's on touch perception in males, I asked the participants what they found to be the softest thing in the world. Young men usually replied "women" in general, but older men almost always said, "A limp penis." In respect to their touch perception of women, I have found that most men comment on the rounded fullness of the women's breasts and—much secondarily—their buttocks. They very seldom mention, however, the wetness of the vagina, although this may be largely a matter of inhibition.

When one partner touches the other, the manner in which the contact is made can express many different things. The *stroking* of the partner involves not only friction, as skin moves across skin, but also form, as the hand follows the curves of the body. To stroke is to define the shaping of the situation, to discover where the partner is in the world. A *caress* is a foreshortened kind of stroking, affectionately reassuring rather than overtly exploratory. People who employ *pinching* during sex are trying to reassure themselves that the other person is truly there by getting a sharp reaction from them. When a person *scratches* another, an attempt is being made to peel away the coverings and literally get under the other person's skin. Because the skin is aroused during coitus as a whole organ, not just at the points where it is being touched, it is a very common experience for people to have an itch during sex, generally in a part of the body that is not being touched at the moment. Thus, many people find it necessary to scratch themselves, lightly, in an almost reflexive way. It is as though all the skin were demanding to be touched in one way or another.

The importance of the sense of touch to our sexuality is emphasized by the fact that it has been utilized to help couples break up rigid body attitudes, to facilitate intimacy, and to overcome sexual difficulties, as in the Masters and Johnson technique of sensate focusing. Most six-year-old children are very much "in touch" with their own bodies, but because children are subsequently discouraged by prohibition from touching themselves intimately, many adults have to be taught the uses and pleasures of the sense of touch all over again.

On one level the sense of touch is profoundly physiological. As an example, massage creates a feeling of well-being not just because it is arousing and tranquilizing at the same time but also because it facilitates the disposal of waste material from the muscles in the area that is being stroked. But as we have seen in regard to the infant's need for being touched, this sense if also connected to our ability to relate to other persons emotionally. It is for this reason that touching has been made a fundamental part of certain approaches to psychotherapy and is used in the encounter movement.

In terms of the love world the importance of touching is twofold. First, it heighens sensual pleasure and accentuates the physicality of the sex act. In the love relationship, however, it takes on another dimension. When two people touch one another in a spontaneous, exploratory, and tender way, a psychological intimacy is created. In certain sexual encounters, as with a prostitute, there will be stimulation as well as a quality of impersonality. The prostitute's actions are not spontaneous but programmed, and her reactions controlled, so that a barrier which makes true intimacy impossible is thrown up. Physical closeness is fundamental to the sense of intimacy between a loving couple, but it must involve a coequal sense of give-and-take in order for the couple to enter fully into the love world.

In terms of sex, the second most important sense is that of smell. It may be a person's visual attractiveness that initially catches our attention, but during sex both touch and smell are more important than vision. We can close our eyes when we make love—and many people do—but we cannot avoid touching and smelling our partner. Through odor one individual is immediately encompassed by another. When you smell another person's odor, that person immediately and literally becomes a mixed-in part of your own existence, for smell involves the perception of the molecules of a substance carried on the air. In the act of smelling one absorbs minute particles of the odor source itself, and thus the very essence of the thing that is being smelled is taken up and perceived.

Smells carry with them certain feelings. For example, fecal smells and earthy smells in general convey a feeling of decomposition and of a concomitant chaos. All odors, of course, are released by the *breakdown* of matter into smaller particles. But it is only the "dark" smells that specifically remind us of this process of decomposition and which may therefore be distressing. Even earthy smells have different effects on different people. The heavy odor of musk, the perfume derived from one of the sex glands of the musk-ox, is sensually exciting to some people but offensive to others. The same is true of sweet smells. One patient of mine has an aversion to sweet perfumes, and sometimes in the close air of a theater he will ask to change places with a friend if he finds himself sitting next to someone who has inundated herself—or himself, these days—with sweet scent. The young man readily acknowledges that the heavy use of sweet perfume reminds him unpleasantly of his mother, an overprotective woman whose all-pervasive influence he has spent many years trying to escape.

Often, of course, we would find it impossible to pinpoint the reasons for liking one smell and disliking another. Such reactions and evaluations are built up over long periods of time and may not be connected with any one occurrence or series of events. But a man who is nauseated by the smell of new-mown grass—an odor pleasing to most—may be fully aware that his reaction is caused by the fact that as a boy he had to mow the lawn every Saturday before being allowed to join his friends at their games. Such associations may affect our response not only to the smell of burning leaves or frying onions but also to the people we choose as our friends and lovers. It is a common experience for us to take note that a childhood friend has married a man who "looks just like her father." At the same time we may be quite unaware that another friend has married a woman who looks nothing like his mother but does in fact *smell* like her.

Our sense of smell is particularly personal, in that no one else can really share in it. Two people can discuss in great detail whey they both find a painting beautiful to look at, but they are likely to find it difficult to get much beyond "It smells delicious" when speaking of a roast chicken. Because odors are all pervasive and are absorbed all at once, it is often hard to be analytic about them.

Our feelings about the odors of other human beings are affected by cultural attitudes. In the United States we tend to be reticent about human odor. Yet in many societies identifying odors are of such importance that rubbing the nose on the face of the loved one is the preferred form of affectionate greeting. The Russian Kakuts and the Laplanders both use this form of greeting. In many parts of Asia, Africa, and Polynesia, as well as among some American aboriginals, the so-called olfactory kiss is used. This "kiss" does not involve touch at all, but only smell.

There are three phases to the olfactory kiss: The nose is first applied close to the cheek of the other person, followed by a long nasal inhalation with lowered eyelids, and in conclusion there is a slight smacking of the lips but without application of the mouth to the cheek. There are tribes in Southeast India who will say to a loved one, "Smell me," rather than "Kiss me." Among the Chinese who employ this type of kiss, it is thought of as an expression of sexuality permissible only between lovers. In some other societies, however, its connotations go beyond the sexual, and it may be used as a greeting among relatives. The olfactory kiss is also used by the American Eskimo and the Blackfeet Indians. There have been theories put forward that the olfactory kiss is related to a primitive stage of development, closer to the animal world, but in fact, a form of this kiss is practiced by many Europeans, including the Russians and the French. In the French language a single verb—*sentir*—means not only to smell but also to feel and to be aware of, with the exact meaning determined by the context.

The sense of smell does not, of course, play as large a part in human sexuality as it does among animals. Lower animal orders are dominated by smell, as shown by the importance of pheromones—hormonal substances that elicit physiological or behavioral response from other members of a given species. Sex is strikingly affected by smell not only among mammals but also among insects and birds. In some species of insect the sense of smell is much more highly developed in the male than the female; the female never leaves her underground burrow but, by protruding part of her anatomy above ground, attracts males with her pungent odor. The splendor of the peacock's tail is only incidentally a visual attraction; its primary function is to produce and disseminate aphrodisiac odors. A strutting peacock is not a vain male flaunting his plumage, but a sexually aroused male attempting to attract the female with his odor.

Animals appear to be sexually affected by the odors of human beings as well. In *The Descent of Man* Darwin recorded that many apes become sexually excited by the odor of human females, a fact that has been confirmed by more recent investigators. It seems that certain women give off odors that are enough like female apes to cause the male anthropoids to "go ape." It is believed that wild animals can be more quickly and effectively trained in captivity by human beings of the opposite sex. It has been noted, for instance, that male lion tamers inspire greater loyalty from lionesses than from lions, while female trainers have the opposite experience.

Despite the powerful part they play in sexual arousal, many people would just as soon ignore—or even cover up—the natural odors of themselves and their partners. When the odors of the body are spoken of in terms of sex, it is usually in a romantic and metaphorical manner. The French symbolist poet Edmond Haraucourt, for instance, writing about his mistress' body in his poem "A Symphony of Scents," describes her breath as smelling of honey, her saliva of sugar, almonds, her neck of chestnut leaves, and her hair of jasmine. Only in reference to her armpits does he describe an actual bodily odor: the sharp tang of warm salt. Both the French and Italian languages have a specific term to describe the erotic odor of a woman—in French, *le parfum de la femme*, in Italian, *odore di femina*. Unsurprisingly, a distinct chauvinism makes itself apparent here since there is no comparable term for the erotic odor of men.

In *Odoratus Sexualis*, the dermatologist and sexologist Iwan Bloch quotes the work of H. Zwaardemaker, who developed a general classification system of odors. Zwaardemaker put all the animal scents with sexual affiliations into one particular group of chemical relationships: the fatty acids of the aliphatic group called the capryls. In this group of caprylic odors belong those of perspiration, vaginal secretions and sperm. Another researcher noted that the odor of semen is also to be found in chestnuts and some thorns.

The odor of the female genitals is not especially pungent except during sexual intercourse and at the time of menstruation. During intercourse secretions increase and the body temperature rises, causing a natural emanation and heightening of odor. But at other times the vagina has a much less powerful scent than does the penis. In both men and women, however, the strongest concentration of caprylic odor occurs in the armpits. The sweat glands and the sebaceous glands (which create the oily substance sebum that lubricates the hair follicles) are particularly large under the arm, and their separate secretions combine to create the strong caprylic odor. Shaving the armpit, as most women do in the United States, cuts down on the sebaceous secretions, but many European women would claim that this practice diminishes a woman's erotic appeal.

In the United States, of course, both men and women have a fear of bodily odors that sometimes borders on the obsessive. The sale of underarm deodorants has been steadily increasing for decades, and in addition, there are now genital deodorants for both men and women on the market. Since most deodorants have a distinctly metallic taste, the manufacturers of genital deodorants have attempted to imbue their products with various aromatic flavors, such as lemon or peppermint, but even so the market for them has remained small.

Humankind has been in the business of producing artificial odors to enhance or disguise the natural body odors for thousands of years. The first known perfumes were developed by Egyptian priests; originally they were used only in religious ceremonies and in the process of embalming the dead. Later, although the making of perfumes continued to be restricted to the

priesthood, it became common to use these scents for
personal adornment, and they were regarded as a sign
of refinement. Shakespeare's description of Cleopatra's
barge—"Purple the sails, and so perfumed that/The
winds were lovesick with them"—is not only beautiful
poetry, but also a fairly accurate picture of the extent
to which perfumes were being used in Egypt during
the first century B.C.

Throughout history, however, there has been a certain suspicion concerning perfumes. In some societies
they were regarded as decadent; in others, they were
associated with witchcraft. The ancient Hebrews,
who learned the art of making perfumes in Egypt, at
first allowed them to be used only by priests. But soon
they were being disseminated more widely, and Judith
is described as wearing perfume when she seduced
Holofernes. In Greece, where for the first time the
manufacture of perfumes was placed in the hands of
women, we find one of the early connections between
perfume and witchcraft. The tragic heroine Medea
was both a perfumer and a sorceress. Julius Caesar—
perhaps in reaction against the wiles of Cleopatra—
prohibited the use of perfumes in Rome but without
much success. A number of the later Roman em-
perors, including Caligula and Nero, were famous for
their lavish hand with them.

Perfumes were greatly appreciated in the Orient
and were brought back to England from the Middle
East by the Crusaders. Elizabeth I doted on them, and
the fashion was taken up by her courtiers, who had
great need for them under the reign of Elizabeth's
successor, James I, a monarch who almost never bathed
and quite simply stank. But a reaction set in against
them, and in 1770 Parliament passed an act making it a
punishable offense for a women to seduce a man into
marriage through the use of scents. In seventeenth-
century France the use of perfumes was so widespread and so extreme that the ladies of the court
disdained bathing, masking their puissant odor by

wearing small sponges soaked with perfume under their armpits and between their thighs. Curiously, the prostitutes of that period were far cleaner than the noble women: for medical reasons, the prostitutes bathed regularly.

Various perfumes have been considered particularly erotic in certain cultures. Musk, the longest-lasting and strongest of perfumes, has for centuries been highly regarded in the East. In the Koran the nymphs who welcome heroes to paradise are portrayed as consisting of pure musk. In our own culture, of course, many women's perfumes and men's colognes are advertised in terms of their supposed sexual allure. But the choice of a perfume remains an extremely subjective matter; it seems likely that most people choose a scent because it mixes well with their natural body odor. The same perfume can smell quite differently when worn by different people, altered by the scent of the wearer. Thus, when we say, "I like your perfume," we are actually responding in some degree to the fragrance of the person and not just to the perfume.

Just as some people respond more keenly to music than do others, some of us have a more acute sense of smell. Even so, there remains a certain mystery as to why we find ourselves sexually responsive to the odor of particular people. Richard K. Champion, an English writer on the subject, quotes from a case history in which a forty-three-year-old man described his sexual relations with his wife:

The one thing she had which no other woman has ever had in my experience, was a wonderful smell. I noticed it the first time we went to bed together and it is very largely responsible that throughout our relationship I have regularly performed cunnilingus on her. You see, the smell is very concentrated between her thighs. It's rather sweet yet spicy. Quite unlike anything else I know. And when she's aroused the smell is considerably strengthened. That's why I prolong cunnilingus so much. I find the smell very arousing and very enjoyable for itself. With other women, I've never enjoyed cunnilingus and the odours around the vagina have never appealed to me.

When this man's wife, who was slightly older than he was, began her menopause, her vaginal odor was modified. While this is a perfectly natural occurence, it greatly dismayed this particular man. The original odor had been so important to his enjoyment of sex that its changed nature filled him with frustration. Other aspects of the marriage had long been troubled, and the loss of the odor that had so aroused him led him to feel that there was no longer anything to sustain the relationship. Obviously this is a somewhat extreme case, but it does serve to indicate how great a part the sense of smell can play in a sexual relationship.

In many cultures there have been popular myths that the size of a man's nose indicates the proportions of his penis. Despite the baselessness of this assumption, a functional relationship does seem to exist between the nose and the sex organs—not in terms of size but in terms of neurophysiological reaction. A number of clinical papers have reported that nosebleeds often occur with great regularity in adolescents of both sexes at the onset of puberty. In some cases this bleeding continues into adulthood, and there are even recorded cases in which young men suffered a nosebleed each time they had sexual intercourse. Some women have nosebleeds when they are menstruating. In both men and women there is occasionally a swelling of the nasal membranes during intercourse that causes difficulty in breathing. And more commonly, a large number of people develop a slightly runny nose when having sex.

The exact cause of these nasal reactions to or connections with genital activity remain to be pinpointed. But there is no question that our sense of smell plays a large part in sexual arousal and enjoyment. For some, the sense of smell becomes all-important, and there are innumerable cases of fetishistic individuals for whom the smell of armpits, underwear, and even feet become the central, if extreme, focus of the sexual experience. For most of us, of course, the sense of smell is just one aspect of sexual pleasure, but an aspect of greater importance than many people realize, often having a profound effect on our choice of partners.

The sense of taste is less important to sex than that of smell, but the two are strongly related. Indeed, some individuals have great difficulty in distinguishing the taste of many foods if they are prevented from smelling them. Phenomenologically tasting is like smelling in that one absorbs all at once the molecules —the basic building structures—of the partner. This experiencing of the partner through taste brings the greatest possible commingling, since a part of the loved one is thus made a part of oneself.

The tongue has the capacity not only to taste but also to probe and lick. Thus it satisfies both the sense of taste and the sense of touch—for the person being touched and for the toucher. With the tip of the tongue, one can touch one's partner with extraordinary delicacy, while the tongue's wetness, granularity, and sinuosity add a new sensual dimension to that touch.

Because of the skin's function as a heat regulator and excretory organ, giving off sweat, the taste of the skin in general is salty. But beyond that fact, there is very little information in the medical or sexual literature concerning the sense of taste in connection with sex. Such references abound in pornographic novels, but they tend to be highly repetitive, sensational catchphrases. However, some facts have emerged from my research with patients. In respect to the genitals themselves, the taste of the penis is generally described as somewhat salty. The taste of the female genitals—which is affected by both the vaginal transudate and the secretions of the Bartholin's glands—is usually described as being lightly alkaline.

The albuminoid taste of semen, which is sometimes swallowed as the result of fellatio, is variously described. One patient stated that there were two successive tastes involved. During the first phase there was a taste reminiscent of fusel oil—fusel oil being the slightly bitter by-product of grain distillery. During the second phase the taste was described as being nut-like. I presume that the initial fusel taste emanated from the Cowper's gland secretions which occur in the urethra of the male during sexual activity. The second component would probably be an admixture of prostatic fluid and semen. However, it is possible that the first taste might be that of the prostatic fluid, and the second that of the seminal vesicle discharge by itself. There are variations in the taste of the semen depending on foods eaten and medications taken. It is also reported that the taste varies from man to man, but whether this is a matter of diet, hormonal balance, or other bodily processes is unknown.

The senses of touch, smell, and taste all require intimate contact with the partner. But our sense of sight enables us to contact and encompass someone while he or she is still at a distance. Thus one may be "in touch" without actually touching. Our initial attraction to another person is usually based on visual appreciation. Many questions have been raised in recent years, however, as to the degree that males and females are sexually stimulated by the sight of the opposite sex. It had long been assumed that the female responded primarily to the physical stimulation of touch, and the male to sexual ideas. Thus it was believed that men were more aroused by visual aspects of the female than women were by sight of the male. In support of this theory there is the fact that fetishism of various kinds is predominantly a male activity. For the bra fetishist, for instance, the mere sight of a woman's bra hanging on a washline could be arousing. But women were not supposed to be aroused even by photographs or statues of the nude male. It was believed that only the sight of an actual lover who had or was getting an erection could cause a woman to be visually excited. The supposed lack of visual arousal or stimulation by sexual ideas alone has been used as a basis for the statement that some women take longer to respond sexually than the average male Actual tactile stimulation was regarded as necessary to bring about full arousal in the female.

Recent investigations, however, have shown that many of these assumptions were misleading or overstated. Modern knowledge and understanding of women's actual sexual responsivity has given us a clearer view. In the past it may indeed have been true that women responded less to visual stimuli, but it seems likely that this "fact" was the result of culturally induced inhibition. Women were taught that they should not be aroused by the sight of the nude male and should not "think" about sex. As a result, men seemed to choose their sexual partners primarily on the basis of visible physical endowments, while women made their choice on the basis of achievement and social class.

Now that the cultural inequities between men and women are being somewhat lessened, a truer picture of feminine psychology is emerging. One recent investigator, Robert Chartham, found a large number of women who claimed to be aroused by the genital bulge in a man's trousers. Certainly this seems to have been true in earlier centuries when men wore codpieces. "Cod" was a term used for the scrotum, and the codpiece initially came into favor because it allowed more room for the genitals when the legs and hips were encased in tight-fitting hose. But as time went on, the codpieces became larger and larger—a kind of male "falsie"—and were highly decorated, lending support to the idea that women will respond visually to sexual display if the cultural milieu encourages such response. At present we seem to be passing through a period of change in this regard. Many women state that they are not aroused by the naked male unless they have already fallen in love with him; but the number who are aroused by the sight of a nude man, even a stranger, appears to be on the increase, especially among younger women who have been less thoroughly conditioned to believe that they should not respond to such visual stimulation.

The sense of vision, in both sexes, is vastly more important in human beings than in the subhuman primates and lower animals orders. Animal psychologists have developed what they call the genital echo theory of attractiveness. When female primates are in heat, the so-called sexual skin on the backside swells and becomes reddish. The area is not covered by hair and is highly visible, so that the swelling acts as a sexual signal to the males. As human beings evolved and assumed an upright position, these sexual signals were turned to the front, where they are even more visible. But while we have evolved in such a way as to make the sexual features of both men and women more visible, we have at the same time developed social rules that forbid the open display of the genitals. Although there are primitive societies in which the adult male goes about naked, women in *all* societies wear some kind of loincloth for most everyday activities.

The degree to which the sight of the female genitals can affect arousal is strikingly demonstrated in the case histories of several of my patients. One man, whom I treated a number of years ago, told me that as a teenager he used to prowl at night through the backyards of neighboring houses, cutting out the crotch area in any pairs of women's underpants he found hanging on washlines. As I interpret it, this behavior was in no way an attempt at mutilation of the female image but rather a way of removing a physical barrier to the sexual experiences the boy had not yet had. He was attempting to "see" through to the vaginas of these women. Because he did not yet have the freedom to satisfy himself in an adult, healthy way, he had to do it in a distorted way, sneaking around at night.

In another situation, I treated first a woman and then a man who at one point had been lovers, and each told me the same story from his or her particular point of view. The woman had great difficulty in developing any feeling for men and often went to sexual extremes in an attempt to break herself of this detachment and inhibition. One day, when she expected to spend some time with her lover, she cut out the crotch of her panties. Seated in a room with him, she gradually and casually spread her legs so that the man could see up her skirt. For the woman, this was one way of trying to break through her inhibitions. For this sexually experienced man, the sudden awareness of the hole that had been cut in her underwear was, as he described it, the most memorable "sexual turn-on" of his entire life. As he sat across from her, he suddenly found himself, visually speaking, in a vaginal world. He cited this experience as an example of the woman's extreme sexual inventiveness, yet for her the act had been not so much an attempt to excite him as to excite herself.

For some people, then, the visual aspects of sex may be so important as to lead to exhibitionistic or voyeuristic behavior. But many others shy away from the visual. In numerous cases the societal rules of modesty have such a strong effect on an individual that he or she will prefer to have intercourse with the lights turned off or else to close the eyes during sex. Darkness acts as a cover-up—the sex act cannot be seen—and therefore, any anxieties generated by the situation can be diminished. One young woman with considerable sexual experience complained about the fact that so many men seemed afraid to even look at her vagina, let alone perform cunnilingus. Clearly there are many men for whom there is something taboo and anxiety-provoking about the vagina, men whose cultural conditioning and sexual conflicts have made it difficult for them to take visual, oral, or olfactory pleasure in a woman's genitals, but who limit themselves instead to tactile pleasure.

However, there is another aspect to the closing of the eyes during sex. Darkness shuts out unnecessary visual distractions and can allow for greater concentration on the other sensual modalities of touch, smell, and taste. For the person who is particularly aroused by odors, the sense of smell will become more acute with the eyes closed. And for some people, it may be easier to enter into the love world with the eyes closed, the darkness creating the feeling of an intensely private world in which only the individual and the loved partner seem to exist.

Light, on the other hand, will be extremely important to lovers who are strongly oriented in their visual sense. Certain sex positions, as we shall see in later chapters, may be adopted particularly because they allow one or both partners to see more of the other's body. As has been pointed out before, the pupils dilate when lovers look into one another's eyes, as they try to encompass one another more completely. Some people keep their eyes open during sex but develop a distant, staring look, as though seeking to see beyond the immediate environment into eternity. One patient of mine complained about his wife's doing just this when they made love. He considered it unromantic and thought it a sign of sexual oddity. He apparently felt that her staring was isolating him from her, that she was concentrating not on him but on something within herself.

Obviously, then, the question of the sense of vision during sex is a complicated one. In general, sight facilitates contact, awareness, and emotional expression. All these factors help create fusion within the love world. Yet for some, entrance into the love world and the achievement of a feeling of transcendence may be more easily accomplished with the eyes closed. But it should be remembered that we all approach sex with highly individualized sets of behavioral responses. If both partners like to have their eyes open or both like to have them closed, it may be easier for them to understand one another. But when partners have developed a relationship in which both feel emotionally secure, there can be a relaxed recognition that while they exist in the love world together, their ways of entering into it may be somewhat different.

The chief importance of our sense of hearing in the sexual encounter involves the use of words and non-verbal utterances as a form of communication between the partners. This subject will be more fully discussed in a later chapter, "Love Songs." At this point let us examine a few other aspects of the aural sense. During intercourse the sense of hearing is the one that remains most in touch with the ordinary world around us. It is the radar system among our senses, alerting us to the possibility of intrusion. As such, our hearing can sometimes distract us from, rather than enhance, our participation in sex. Is that the children stirring? we may suddenly wonder. Or the phone may ring. When it does, most people will try to ignore it. Yet it is impossible not to wonder who is calling, and the rhythm of coitus is likely to be broken until the ringing stops. The partners' absorption in one another is mitigated by outside sounds; they are jolted out of the love world and back into mundanity. Eternity dissolves, and a sense of nowness reasserts itself. A ringing phone or doorbell can even cause some men to lose their erections; once the distraction is eliminated, the attempt to coalesce with the partner must begin all over again.

In terms of enhancement, the most common use of the aural sense (aside from registering the words and sounds uttered by the couple) is through the playing of music while making love. The question is: What kind of music? The power of music to move human beings is very great, but a score that one person finds beautiful may have a very different effect on someone else. One young woman reported playing a record of medieval religious chants, which she put on the stereo just as she and her lover were getting into bed. To her the music was soothing and transcendent; but to the man, who had been brought up in a strict religious household, it was extremely disturbing. In his view, the young woman began to realize, sex and religion were in contradiction with one another, and he could not perform sexually while this aural reminder of his religious background continued.

In another case a couple thought it would be exciting to make love to the insistent and accelerating musical rhythm of Ravel's *Bolero*. But they discovered that the beat of the music was so controlled that in trying to keep pace with it, they lost all sense of spontaneity. They could not lose themselves in one another but found themselves *performing* to the music. Again, the love unity could be achieved only by removing the source of aural overstimulation. Thus, while music can enhance sex for some people, the choice of the piece to be played should be carefully considered in respect to its potential for distraction rather than enhancement.

There are two further, less commonly discussed senses which have particular relevance in terms of sex. First, there is the sense of gravity. From birth we make some of our assumptions about the world we live in on the basis of our sense of gravity. Through the appropriate sensory organs of the nervous system the infant determines whether the outside world is to be trusted or feared by direct contact with the person holding it. The person who clutches a baby as though afraid of dropping it will give the infant an entirely different kind of message about the world from the person who cradles the child gently. From the way it is held, the social anthropologist Ashley Montagu writes, "The infant makes the proper discriminations in much the same way as adults do when they draw inferences about the character of a person from the quality of his handshake."

As we mature, our feelings about gravity will affect our willingness to live in high-rise apartments, our preferences for mountain climbing, golf or sailing, our fear of or pleasure in flying. And it will also affect our preferences in sex positions. For some people, it may be important to feel that they are supported by the ground, causing them to avoid a sexual situation in which they are in a vertical rather than a horizontal position. One person may enjoy the sense of buoyancy provided by the water bed, while another is disturbed by the sense of tidal shifting under them.

Closely allied to the sense of gravity is the kinesthetic sense. Side-to-side rocking movements, in-and-out rapid thrusting movements, and slow, rotational grinding movements—all are applications of the kinesthetic sense. We know that rocking in childhood serves as a reassurance in that it duplicates the soothing rhythms of the fetus in the womb; in one case history we have seen how a child abruptly deprived of the rocking he cherished was affected even into adulthood. As with all the other senses, there are aspects of our sense of gravity and our kinesthetic sense that are experienced by each of us in unique, intensely personal ways. The significance of that fact will become of central concern in the next several chapters as we begin to explore the sex positions.

CHAPTER 5

Common Sex Positions

How many sex positions are there?

The answer to this question will depend, of course, on the criteria used to define the differences between one position and another. Oriental literature abounds in works on the subject, many of them dating back to ancient times. One of the most logical and at the same time comprehensive of these treatises is by the ancient Chinese "Master of the Cave Profound," as he called himself. "Examining the postures of intercourse," he wrote, "there are no more than thirty ways." But he goes on to describe nine *styles* of intercourse based on the slowness or quickness of the action and the rhythm and direction of the movement involved. Each of these styles can be used with any one of the thirty positions so that when positions and styles are multiplied together, there are nearly 300 possible patterns of sexual intercourse.

Some sex manuals describe even more sex positions. Many of these variants involve only differences in the placing of the legs or arms. In addition, many of the listed variations depend on the use of props—chairs, stools, swings—as is also the case with many of the positions described in Oriental manuals. The placing of arms and legs or the use of props can have definite significance, as we shall see. But significance is the crucial word here. It is not number of positions that I am concerned with but rather the phenomenological *meaning* of those positions and the ways in which they reflect the essential behavioral structure of individual human beings.

From the phenomenological point of view there are four basic positions, each of which must be looked at from the perspective of both participants, the female and the male. All other positions—and indeed, there are hundreds of possibilities—are variations on these basic four. Some of the variations are so subtle as to be of little import in expressing the basic couple orientation, while others are far more telling and do indicate a substantial modification in the significance of the basic position. In this chapter I will be dealing with the four basic positions. A subsequent chapter will be devoted to the variations, some of them quite imaginative. In my examination of the unusual but not infrequent positions, I will present a range of several dozen variants that will allow couples to analyze on their own any additional configurations.

In *Sleep Positions* I dealt with the individual's bodily relationship to the geography of the bed, the fundamental terrain of the sleep world. Only in terms of couple sleep was the additional element of the relationship to the partner discussed. Here, however, I will be concentrating on the relationship between the sexual partners, on how the bodily attitudes of the couple during intercourse reflect their overall everyday relationship and indicate each partner's individual requirements for entering into the love world.

It is important to make clear from the outset that the significance of a particular position derives from its being *preferred*. Some couples may almost always use a single preferred position during sex. Others may experiment more freely and assume a considerable variety of positions depending on mood, situation, or level of excitement. But even those couples who experiment to a large degree will return time and again to one or two positions that most explicitly delineate their couple relationship. Moreover, from the case histories I will be using as illustrations it becomes evi-

dent that even in the course of experimenting it is the
positions most closely related to the basic preferred
position that give the greatest satisfaction to the couple and allow them to enter most thoroughly into the
love world.

Beyond the matter of the specific positions that are
preferred, I will be considering the question of which
partner initiates sex as well as who determines the pace
and rhythm of the sexual activity pattern once it has
begun. There is, as we shall see, a correspondence between the choice of position and these other elements
of the sexual equation. Finally, I will be relating the
chosen positions to the elements of intimacy, spontaneity, physicality, commitment, and pleasure that
must be dealt with in every love-sex relationship.

It should be made clear from the outset that each of
the basic positions admits of many variations. Major
variations, which change the configurations in highly
significant ways, will be treated in the next chapter.
But within any particular basic position there are of
course a great many minor bodily adjustments that
may be made by a given individual or couple. So long
as these adjustments do not alter the *basic configuration*, the fundamental meaning of the position is not
altered either. If the basic configuration is changed,
though, then a different position has been created and
must be analyzed in this light.

The first of the four basic positions, and the pre-
dominant one in our culture, is the so-called missionary position. The origin of the popular name for this
position is reported by Bronislaw Malinowski in his
study of native cultures of the Southwest Pacific.
These South Sea islanders commonly used a position
in which the man squatted facing the woman, who lay
supine with her thighs over the man's thighs. They
were amused and fascinated by the white foreigners
who first came to their islands and would spy on the
activities of the whites, who were usually missionaries.

Missionary

The islanders found the white people's way of making love, with the woman supine and the man prone on top of her, extremely curious and dubbed it the missionary position.

Let us look at the missionary position phenomenologically, first from the woman's perspective. Lying on her back, the woman is supported by the earth (or bed) in a relaxed horizontal position. At the same time, however, she must to a considerable extent support the weight of the man above her. The woman is thus enclosed from all sides, cradled by the bed and enveloped by the man's body. Her ability to move her torso is limited by the weight of the man, although her arms are free to embrace or caress him. She does have the ability to move her hips and pelvis, provided that her legs are spread, with the man between them. The degree of pelvic leverage will depend on whether her legs are flat on the bed surface or raised; the greatest degree of pelvic thrust is obtained when the knees are sharply flexed but with the feet remaining flat on the bed.

In some feminine circles the missionary position is associated with a pejorative sense of submissiveness, even inferiority. It is seen almost as a metaphorical embodiment of the position of women in life in general:

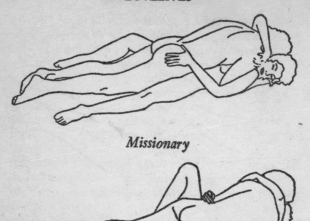

Missionary

Missionary

The man is on top, and the woman's freedom of movement is limited. Nevertheless, in spite of the growth of liberationist thinking, women's responses to questions concerning preferred sexual positions show that this position is still preferred above all others. There is, however, a definite split between different types of respondents interviewed, showing that for some women the missionary position is far more active than it is for others.

The first type of woman is the generally passive one. She usually allows the man to initiate sexual activity. She also allows him to determine the pattern of movement during intercourse—the tempo, the kind of thrusting employed—while she lies accepting his direction in the sexual sphere, just as she does in their relationship as a whole. Somewhat surprisingly this kind of woman has multiple orgasms of the so-called squeak variety. The term "squeak" is often used by my female patients to describe this kind of orgasm. More technically, according to the major classifications of women's orgasmic reaction patterns, this kind of woman will begin to have orgasms of low amplitude but rapid frequency almost from the beginning of the plateau phase. In some women such orgasms begin even earlier, during the arousal phase. These orgasms are also sometimes described by women as being composed of tiny bubbles or of small explosions like a string of firecrackers.

During my research for *Sleep Positions* I found that women who sleep in the full fetal position, curled in upon themselves, sometimes clutching a pillow to them, reported having orgasms of the multiple squeak type. Further interviewing has shown that the full fetal sleeper is generally a woman who also prefers the missionary position and allows the man to control the sexual pattern. This type of woman tends to be relatively unrealized in terms of her overall life potentials, a person who likes to be held, protected, and taken care of.

The second type of woman preferring the missionary position shows quite a different personality pattern and is a more active participant in intercourse. These women are responsible for the initation of intercourse about 50 percent of the time; they also initiate changes in the coital activity pattern about half the time, rather than let the man assume complete charge. Such women appear to be both more experienced and more responsive in the sexual area than the first type. One woman stated that she did not feel at all passive in the missionary position. She responded to her husband's thrusts with equal pelvic movement of her own, finding the missionary position preferable because it gave her the greatest clitoral stimulation. Like most women of this second type, she usually experiences orgasm as one "big bang." This kind of orgasm is found to be completely satisfying by these women. One woman stated that although she could have multiple orgasms, she did not strive to achieve them and found them no more fulfilling than a single explosive one.

The third type of woman stating a preference for the missionary position is distinguished from the other two types chiefly by the nature of her orgasm and by the fact that she is more likely to enjoy the variety of assuming an alternate position at least some of the time, usually the female-astride position in which the man is recumbent. This third type has orgasms of the big-bang type, but in multiples rather than singly. The multiple orgasms usually number four to eight, with no general pattern as to which of the individual orgasms is the most pleasurable. Both the second and third types of woman generally show themselves as living in two styles: a period of intense exertion and activity, followed by a phase of great relaxation. This phasic pattern is somewhat more profound in women of the third type, as might be expected from their occasional use of the woman-astride position. Such personalities are sometimes passive, sometimes assertive. This is clearly illustrated in the case of one woman who prefers the missionary position because she likes the feeling of being enveloped by the man, yet at the same time it is she who sets the rhythm pattern, with her husband taking his cues from her.

An examination of these three types of women shows that it is, in fact, incorrect to stereotype the missionary position as a "submissive" one so far as the woman is concerned. It can indeed be a very passive position. But for many women, among the second and third types, this position is not experienced as passive at all. They respond in purely physical terms as actively as their husbands or lovers, sometimes even setting the pace of the sexual encounter themselves, at least among women of the third type.

There is an additional factor that clearly influences the preference for the missionary position expressed by these women. Many of them spoke of the importance of having a feeling of tenderness and love during intercourse, and the close face-to-face contact that is physically effected by the missionary position obviously enhances the sense of emotional intimacy between the couple. It has been pointed out before that in the evolution of the human species there is a distinct divergence, in terms of the placement of the genitals, from the anatomical structure of primates. The movement of the genitals toward the front of the body increases the importance of vision in sex and makes it possible for human beings to look into one another's eyes and mutually embrace one another during copulation. Even for those who prefer to keep their eyes closed, the face-to-face orientation of the missionary position facilitates kissing. Both the genitals and the mouths of the partners may be closely interlocked, increasing the sense of intimacy and of unity between the partners in sex, as in their lives as a whole. It was exactly this intimacy, of course, that the Pacific islanders who gave the position its name were trying to avoid. In these societies love was repressed, for reasons that have already been explained, and by squatting above the woman with his torso at right angles to her, the man prevented himself from getting too "close" to the woman in all senses of the word. The missionaries themselves, of course, were involved in trying to "convert" these islanders to the standards and outlook of the Western culture from which the missionaries came. Thus for an islander to be considered truly converted, that person would have to embrace not only the religious code of the missionaries but also the sexual partner in the preferred Western form.

In the last few pages I have been describing three general types of women who prefer the missionary position. But it should be remembered that the delineation of these types is based on the responses of many *individual* women. Although a given woman's expression of her preferences, together with her state-

ments concerning her orgasmic pattern, will make it
clear that she is of a particular type, each woman remains a unique person. The very fact that the assumption of the missionary position is experienced in
different ways by different women and involves varying degrees of activity and initiative demonstrates the
fact that *all* aspects of a given position must be considered if the uniqueness of the particular individual is
to be understood. At the same time, however, it must
be emphasized that while the various aspects will
clarify and refine the overall picture, they seldom
contradict one another. Where contraditions do appear, they are expressive of contradictions that exist in
the total life situation of the person.

For instance, a woman whom I shall call Margo was
married to a man who was the son of a wealthy self-
made industrialist. The husband, Alan, worked for his
father and—as often occurs in these cases—sometimes
found it difficult to measure up to expectations. Alan
wanted to play the dominant and assertive role that
was expected of him in life, and at times he succeeded.
But then there would be periods in which things
would go badly, and he would feel inept, despondent,
and a failure. In their lovemaking Alan and Margo
both generally preferred the missionary position, although Margo regarded herself as being very active in
this configuration, alternating the control of the
rhythmic pace at times with her husband. She found,
however, that whenever Alan was having difficulties
with his father and was unable to hold onto the aggressive role, his sexual drive would diminish. At such
times she would occasionally take the woman-astride
position, assuming command of the sexual situation.
Yet she was always content to return to the missionary position when her husband's ability to assume
dominance reasserted itself.

Thus we can see that Margo was a woman of the
third type: She had both passive and assertive elements in her way of living. In general, she preferred

to have her husband on top, and in this position she would synchronize her own activity with his pelvic thrusting. Significantly Alan regularly discussed his business problems with her, and in this area, too, she would contribute her own point of view. When Alan was at low ebb, Margo had reserves that made it possible for her to take charge actively, acting as a temporary surrogate. She would tease his father on social occasions, now standing in for the retreating husband. By this example she showed her husband that it was possible to stand up to the father figure and get away with it. And she would assume responsibility in the sexual sphere as well when necessary. It might seem that her assertiveness in these circumstances would make her husband feel even more uncertain, but in fact, her example appeared to motivate him toward renewed efforts to regain his sense of male identity and control over challenging situations.

Let us now look at the missionary position from the male point of view. The fact that this position involves the greatest possible degree of face-to-face intimacy usually contributes to a man's choice of this position to some extent, although this factor does not play as large a part in men as in women. For men, cultural stereotypes appear to have a great influence in choosing the missionary position. Just as most women were taught that they should be sensitive, dependent, and submissive and play a nurturing role focused on the home and the family, so men were taught that they should be aggressive, dominant, and competitive, playing an independent role concentrated on the hard, practical world of commerce. Thus many men simply do not feel "masculine" unless they are on top of the woman during coitus, demonstrating in a physical way the dominance they have been taught to believe is their prerogative.

These role stereotypes are changing, of course, as the recognition grows that it is possible for a man *or* a woman to be *both* assertive and sensitive, independent and nurturing. Yet the traditional concepts of male and female roles retain their impact for a great many people. Thus, for the majority of men, when a position other than the missionary is preferred, there are usually very strong reasons for it, as we have already seen, for instance, in the case of the man described in the first chapter who preferred the rear-entry position because he felt claustrophobic unless he was periscopically able to see all around him. The missionary position is not, in fact, the most dominating position that a man can assume, but it appears to conform most comfortably with the stereotyped male self-image. Men who do assume other positions do so either out of strong need or because they are sufficiently assured of their masculinity that it does not disturb them to accommodate the woman's strong desire for another position.

The position that is most "passive" for men from a phenomenological point of view is the woman-astride position in which the man lies on his back and the woman straddles his body. For women, riding the man is the most assertive of the basic positions. The woman-astride position was the one most commonly preferred in ancient Greece, and its use was also very common in ancient China and Japan. While these cultures allowed women little or no political power, the female reigned supreme in the home, being on top, as it were, in family matters.

In our culture women who prefer or insist on having intercourse in the woman-astride position are generally quite assertive. The woman who initiates sex, prefers the astride position, determines the coital activity pattern, and usually has one orgasm of the big-bang kind is, in my opinion a predominantly assertive type. Some women who prefer the astride position, however, are of the compulsive type who feel threatened if they do not have control; often their orgasms will be multiple when in the astride position.

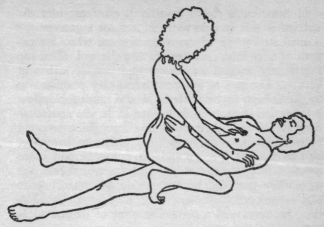

Woman Astride

One woman specifically stated that the position she preferred depended on how aggressive she felt. Usually she preferred the missionary position but sometimes would take the woman-astride position. Only when she was feeling extremely aggressive, however, was she able to have an orgasm while on top.

One woman preferred being astride because it gave her the greatest feeling of control over the sexual encounter. Many years ago she had had an intense orgasm while being masturbated by a male. It frightened her, and ever since her orgasm has been inhibited; she enjoys it but makes a conscious effort to keep it muted. Predictably this woman likes the missionary position least of any. A woman who was having an affair with an older man began to take the woman-astride position because she was told that it was easier for an older man to keep his erection in this position. Significantly, however, after both had achieved orgasm, she liked to turn over into the missionary position with which she was more comfortable and familiar. This change allowed her to relax more completely during the resolution phase.

In most cases the man who prefers to have the woman astride is a person who refuses to accept the normal stereotype of the masculine sex role. One patient of mine who preferred having the woman on top felt deeply anxious about asserting himself in life in general. The idea of using the missionary position was so threatening to him that he would immediately lose his erection if he tried to assume it. In the course of therapy he went through a long struggle attempting to take the missionary position, gradually becoming able to tolerate it more and more. But he had other defenses in reserve, and although he would take the missionary position, he found that his sexual desire and capacity for pleasure were diminished; in addition, he developed a certain amount of genital anesthesia.

With therapeutic work, as he conquers his problems, this man has broken through so that the anesthesia is somewhat overcome. He now allows himself to feel genital sensation, but not in the nerve-rich glans that is most stimulated during the arousal and plateau phases. Rather, it is felt primarily at discharge in the basal part of the penile shaft. In other words, it is only as he enters the love world at orgasm that he will now allow himself to feel genital sensation. Although this is a somewhat extreme case, it does serve to show how profoundly reflective of personality the chosen position can be. Thus this man could not be satisfied in a position that was at odds with himself as a man, and it is only as he has changed in his life as a whole that he has found it possible to feel some genital sensation in the new position.

Even when the woman is astride, however, most men remain quite active. One woman patient with a rich and varied sexual history told me that in her long career she had encountered only one man who was able to be completely inactive and passive with her astride. A man who is much taller than his wife stated that he was forced to take the supine position because of his wife's objection that in the missionary position he was too heavy and smothered her. He had strong feelings about his loss of the stereotyped masculine role but was sufficiently passive so that he was willing to give it up at his wife's insistence.

In fact, many men who are willing to assume the supine position because of the woman's desire to be on top nevertheless manage to effect a compromise that still allows them to assert themselves at some point during intercourse. The relationship between one husband and wife clearly demonstrates this kind of mutual acquiescence. Because of an early sexual trauma, a repressive background, and special circumstances in her life, the wife had developed attitudes of mistrust toward men and had to be rigidly in control of her relationships with them, although she could also at times be submissive and accommodating if she chose. She could have an orgasm only in the woman-astride position, as would be expected. But after she had her orgasm, the husband would reverse positions with her and have his orgasm in the missionary position. At the time I was treating the husband, the act of rolling over to achieve his own orgasm had taken on added significance since he was at the time involved in a battle with his wife over his need to establish more of a sense of his own independence.

One man used the same general pattern in his sexual relationship with women, but in addition, he would help women achieve their orgasm by masturbating them while they were astride. He would masturbate them just to the point of orgasm, and then they would reverse positions. The man took great pride in playing the role of efficient lover and always insisted on having a hand in helping his female partner in life—in more ways than one. Yet when it came to the point of orgasm, it was necessary for him to reverse positions so that he was on top.

In another case an opposite situation existed. The wife found the missionary position the most satisfac-

tory one for the first phase of intercourse. The deep
thrust possible in this position aroused her more completely. But after she had one orgasm in the missionary position, her husband, who generally determined
positions and patterns, would ask her to get on top,
where she continued to have orgasms while he had his.

These last three cases all demonstrate a fundamental
fact concerning intercourse between partners whose
basic requirements for entering the love world are different from one another's: It is always possible in sexual intercourse to have the best of both worlds. If the
couples are in good sexual communication with one
another, the needs of each can be satisfied by changing position at crucial moments. These changes are
clearly not just a matter of whim or variety; they are
based on the most deep-seated characterological needs
of the persons involved. Such sexual compromises
generally reflect a willingness to make compromises in
other areas of the relationship as well, even though
there may be considerable tension and an ongoing
struggle to achieve individual self-satisfaction. If the
couple is willing to compromise in terms of sex positions, it is also usually true that an accord can be
reached in other important areas of their life together.
It should be particularly noted that the importance of
changing position to achieve orgasm took on greater
significance for the man in the first case at a point in
the couple relationship when he was striving for an
increased sense of selfhood.

Aside from the basic fact that the woman is on top
of the man in the astride position, there are other phenomenological matters to be considered. The couple
are facing one another (the position in which the
woman faces away from the man will be discussed in
the next chapter), but there is a greater distance between the faces of the partners. While it is possible
for the partners to kiss in this position without losing
genital contact, the strain involved in doing so limits
the duration of such kisses. There is also less skin con-

tact between the couple than in the missionary position. In overall terms, then the woman-astride position reflects less emotional intimacy and decreased unity between the man and the woman. On the other hand, the man's visual contact with the woman's body is heightened. He can see her breasts and genitals. He can use his hands to fondle her breasts, her buttocks, and her genitals. Physicality may thus be enhanced, particularly for the man. Indeed, the man for whom the use of the hands is particularly important may be greatly stimulated by this position, as in the case of my patient who prided himself on his expertise and liked to masturbate his partner.

The position in which the woman has least control and in which the man is most dominant is the rear-entry position, where the woman kneels or lies and the man inserts his penis into her vagina from behind. Men and women who prefer this position are usually quite guarded in their personalities, fearful of closeness, and prefer not to face one another but to make contact through the genitals alone. For the man, this is an aggressive position, in which he is in greatest control. He sees the woman, but she does not see him. At the same time, as we have noted, his extended visual horizon keeps him more completely in touch with the world around him. For the man too, there is no face-to-face contact, with the genital connection being paramount. The man can play with the woman's breasts, thighs, and genitals as he reaches around her, but for both man and woman, such fondling takes place at a slight remove. Of all the basic positions, this is the most impersonal for both man and woman. This position was the preferred one for ancient Egyptians. It is also widely used among Eskimo groups, where its impersonality may have connections with the Eskimo custom of offering the favors of the wife to honored visitors.

A woman patient who has always guarded herself

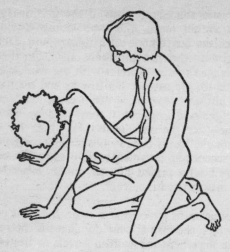

Rear Entry

Rear Entry

in her relationships to men greatly prefers the rear-entry position. She finds the missionary position uncomfortable, although most women who prefer it speak of it as the most "relaxed" position. The woman-astride position appeals to her, but she often finds it physically painful. She states that she does not like the missionary position because it makes her feel "pinned down." Of course, in the rear-entry position she is surrendering even more control to the man, but she does not have to face him, to relate to him directly. In the rear-entry position she becomes greatly excited, her entire body twitching at orgasm, which is usually of the big-bang type.

The great pleasure that this woman derives from having intercourse in the rear-entry position brings up a point that must not be forgotten: No one position is, in the final consideration, "better" than another. So long as the individual finds the position pleasurable and is able to enter the love world through its use, then that position is obviously "right" in terms of that person's life. The positions do reflect the individual's overall ways of living in the world, but just as all of us have certain strengths and weaknesses, so the different positions afford varying *kinds* of pleasure—not necessarily varying *degrees* of pleasure. In the case of the woman just described, the important fact in terms of her sexual fulfillment is that she has found the position that allows her to enjoy sex greatly without arousing her anxieties concerning men.

Men who prefer the rear-entry position usually like to be in control, to initiate sex, to dominate the sexual pattern. Often they want to keep maximum emotional distance from the woman. Of course, as has been noted before, some individuals have more than one preferred position. For instance, one man states that he uses the rear-entry position with his wife only when they have sex in the morning, on first awakening. He sometimes finds himself particularly aroused in the morning—presumably as a result of the concen-

tration of REM (rapid eye movement) periods during
the last phases of sleep, during which erections are
normal occurrences. His wife is more of a night owl
than he is and has a tendency to sleep later and to be
more fatigued in the morning. Thus, when they have
sex in the morning, he approaches her from the rear,
initiating the sex and controlling its pattern, and is at
this point more involved in the love world than she is.

Thus different positions may be used at different
times by the same couple to express the dominant element in their relationship at that particular juncture.
Some couples become involved in conscious sexual experimentation, trying every position in the book in
much the same way that a gourmet cook will attempt
a series of different recipes using similar ingredients.
This is a subject I will be returning to in the next
chapter. But for most couples, the initiation of a new
or seldom-used position, occurring "spontaneously"
and without reference to sex manuals, often reflects a
new or changing element in their relationship as a
whole at that time. If the new position is subsequently
used quite often or comes to be preferred, its significance increases.

Aside from the conscious experimenters, most people
will resist positions that are not congruent with how
they feel about themselves and their partners. A man
who feels strongly about his stereotypical masculine
self-image will not easily or happily adopt a position
in which the woman is in control, for instance. Occasionally a couple will adopt a new position because of
some fundamentally physical reason. This might occur
during a woman's pregnancy or because of a bad
back, a broken limb, or some illness suffered by one
of the partners. Yet mentally this new position will be
regarded as a substitute rather than a preference.

Among couples seeking therapy there are often
struggles for dominance, including the question of
who will be on top and who will be on the bottom
during sexual intercourse. I have sometimes suggested

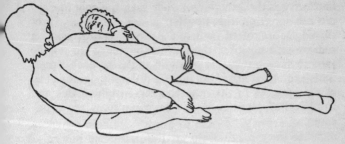

Side Position

to such couples that they try a neutral position, such as the fourth basic one, the side-by-side position. Such suggestions have always been rejected. These couples were involved in a battle for domination of the relationship. Sometimes one might win, sometimes the other. One would be satisfied but not the other. But the compromise of the side-by-side position could give neither of them satisfaction. Now, in fact, I would suggest to such couples that they begin in one position and finish in the other, a compromise that would allow each partner a chance at his or her preferred position for part of the time.

The side-by-side position, in which each partner lies on one side facing the other, is the least common and the most "democratic" of the basic positions. It is a cooperative position, in which control is mutually shared. Indeed, by the very fact that the hip and thigh on the recumbent side of each partner are somewhat restricted in terms of movement, it is almost necessary that the couple be equally involved in thrusting toward one another. The partners are face to face, each has a free hand with which to caress the other's back and buttocks—something that cannot be done to the same mutual degree in any of the other basic positions—and there is maximum skin contact. There is emotional intimacy, a commitment to mutual control, and a high degree of physicality. Since this kind of democratic mutuality is the exception rather than the rule in couple relationships, this position is not commonly preferred. More often, when a patient reports using a side-by-side position, the partners involved do not lie face to face but rather at right angles to each other. This exotic variation has quite a different significance, as we shall see in the next chapter, in which this and many other variants on the basic positions are explicated.

CHAPTER 6

Variations—Standard and Exotic

Even the most exotic sex position is in some way only a variation on one of the four basic positions that have already been described. Some of the possible variations are so commonly used as to be habitual preferred positions; others are sufficiently extreme in their phenomenological configurations, involving such a degree of physical strain for one or both partners that they are unlikely to be used more than occasionally. Some of the most exotic positions come close to contradicting the pattern of the basic position from which they have evolved, but that seeming contradiction is itself of significance.

A number of my patients have stated that although they have distinct preferences in terms of the basic positions, they find that when they are extremely excited, "anything goes." What they mean by "anything goes," however, demands some clarification. From the exotic positions that have been reported to me, it seems clear that while an individual may be willing to bend himself or herself into some quite extraordinary bodily attitudes, these extreme positions nevertheless tend to reflect fundamental life patterns stretched to their limit. Thus, even when a person gets "carried away," it is generally in a particular direction, a direction that is in line with that person's basic orientation to life.

Once again it should be emphasized that I am talking about spontaneously assumed exotic positions, not those that are assumed in a conscious attempt to have sex in every position that can be conceived. In fact, a couple who work their way through a sex manual, trying position 37 on Tuesday and position 38 on Wednesday, are indicating that their fundamental everyday relationship is based on moment-to-moment stimulation, rather than extended interpersonal commitment, and shows that they are searching for ways in which to establish or reestablish deep personal contact. Indeed, most couples trying new positions in response to the stimulation of a sex manual will "experiment" with those positions that in one way or another reflect some aspect of their whole relationship, while completely ignoring other suggested positions.

In presenting the standard variations and exotic positions in this chapter, I will be dealing with several concrete kinds of phenomenological data. Are the partners facing one another, thus showing intimacy? Which partner is bearing the physical weight of the position? Is the partner bearing the physical weight supporting the other or being dominated by the other? What degree of skin contact is involved? What distance between the partners exists? Which of the senses are most involved in the position, and which are least brought into play? Are the hands free to caress the partner or are they subjugated only to a supportive and holding role? All these elements enter into the phenomenological import of these positions, although one element may be crucial in one case and of secondary interest in another.

As might be expected, the variations on the missionary position tend to be more "conservative," less exotic and less gymnastic than either the female-astride or rear-entry variations. The most common variation on the missionary position—one used by many couples—is usually called by the French word *Flanquette*. In this position the woman is not completely supine but lies somewhat on one side. The man is above her,

Flanquette

but instead of having both his legs between her thighs, one leg is placed outside one of her thighs and the other inside. It is thus necessary for the woman to lie turned slightly to the side so that genital contact may be made between the partners. This position affords increased contact between the penis and the clitoris. Aside from this physiological advantage, however, the position involves a greater equality of the lower limbs and hips of the partners; the woman is no longer in the totally supine missionary position but is more intermingled with her partner. Since one of her hips is lifted off the bed surface, this position also allows the woman somewhat more mobility. This position is moving in the direction of a side-by-side position, yet the man remains on top.

Another often employed variant of the missionary position conveys a very different phenomenological message. The woman lies flat on her back with her legs raised almost at a right angle to her torso, placing her feet over the man's shoulders as he kneels with her buttocks between his thighs. The partners are face to face, but the ability to kiss may be curtailed since the woman's legs act as a barrier between the upper bodies of the partners. There is lessened skin contact than in the usual missionary position, and the man's freedom to fondle the woman is diminished since he is likely to need one hand to brace himself against the

Locomotive

bed surface. The woman can caress the man's face or chest and hold his waist or thighs, but she cannot clasp him to her. The man in this position is very active; deep, aggressive penetration is facilitated. This position, which I call the *Locomotive*, has recently been adopted by a couple whose life together is undergoing a period of stress, with many major changes imminent in their overall situation. The wife is particularly concerned by this period of flux, and it is she who instigated the use of this position, finding that the assertiveness of her husband in this position gives her a sense of reassurance as to his strength and solidity.

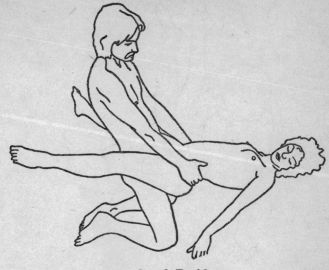

South Pacific

In the *South Pacific* position the woman is throwing herself into the man's arms. He accommodates her but remains with upright torso, denying full intimacy. This position is similar in many respects to the one used by the Pacific islanders who found the standard face-to-face "missionary" position so strange.

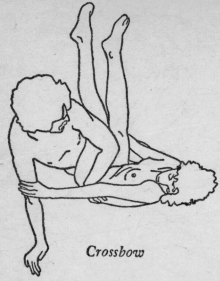

Crossbow

The *Crossbow* position places the man at cross-purposes with the woman. Even though he is on top of the situation, he penetrates the woman at a 90-degree angle. The tangential aspects of this position, and the difficulty of achieving visual contact, show an unwillingness on the part of the man to approach the woman too closely.

Slingshot

In the *Slingshot* position the man supports himself above the woman. She is passive but does not bear the weight of the man. There is no intermingling of the lower body and minimum skin contact. This is a highly visual position for the man, since he is able to see all of the woman's torso as well as the genital juncture.

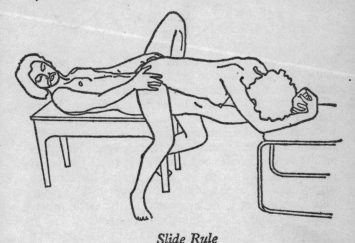

Slide Rule

The *Slide Rule* is a position in which both partners are supported by inanimate objects rather than by each other. Stretched between hassocks, the man and the woman are heading in opposite directions. She appears to be pulling away, while the man retains a superficial hold on her. The fact that his feet are both placed on the ground shows an attempt to retain control, but male dominance is here stretched almost to the breaking point.

The partners are also heading in opposite directions in the *Hinge* position. The upper parts of their bodies are out of contact, and there is a total lack of visual

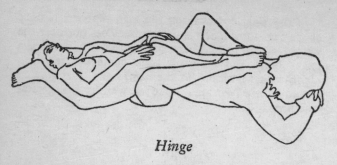

Hinge

intimacy—each partner seems absorbed in a private world. But there is good genital contact and the position is a more tactile one than the Slide Rule.

The *Vine* is a position in which the woman is extremely dependent on the man. He kneels above her with his back straight, supporting himself with both arms. The woman plants both feet alongside his calves on the surface of the bed (or floor), raises her pelvis to meet his, and wraps her arms around his torso to support herself as she brings her upper torso against him. Only her feet remain rooted to the earth; otherwise, she clings to him like a vine to an arbor. But in addition to the dependency shown in this position, there is also evidence of a passionate desire for unity, with the woman lifting herself free of the earth to merge with the man above her.

It is interesting that in the Vine position both the legs and the arms of the two partners are virtually immobilized. During intercourse the ability of the hands to caress, fondle and stroke increases both the intimacy and the physicality of coitus. They can express tenderness with great subtlety and finesse; they can be used to clasp possessively or to scratch aggressively. Thus when they are immobilized by the necessity of being used for support, one important mode of communication between the partners is removed. Of course, if the hands are free and are not used but are allowed to lie loosely at the sides, their lack of involvement can indicate passivity and lack of commitment to the partner. If they are stretched above the head, in an attitude of surrender, an even more profound passivity is shown. But they can also be thrown back in ecstasy, the muscles taut and the fingers stretched; this happens particularly at orgasm and demonstrates both abandonment to the partner and an attempt to reach out to infinity as the love world is fully entered.

The legs also are expressive of the relationship between the partners, although their connotations are less complex and less finely turned than those of the hands. In the missionary position the degree to which the woman's thighs are spread gives an obvious sign of her receptivity. If the knees are flexed, with the soles of the feet planted on the surface of the bed, the woman will have greater pelvic leverage and gives evidence of more active genital participation, sometimes controlling the rhythm of the genital activity pattern as much as or more than the man. As we have seen, when the woman's legs are raised high in the air,

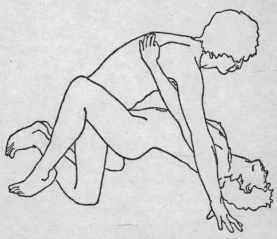

Vine

placed over the shoulders of the man, some of this mobility is lost. From the man's point of view, when the knees are in contact with the bed, as in the Locomotive position, he is showing great assertiveness. At orgasm the man may change position, extending his legs straight out, reaching with all his body. The intertwinement of the partner's legs shows a greater equality and desire to merge.

The use of the legs takes on a different kind of significance when the couple are actually standing as they engage in intercourse. The *Ten Cents a Dance* position illustrates this difference. The woman stands with her back against the wall, while the man faces her with his legs between hers. The woman is heavily supported by the wall, but there is much skin contact between the couple and close face-to-face intimacy. Although the assumption of the standing position frees both partners from the inertia of the horizontal missionary position, the woman still feels pinned against the supporting wall. The shift from the horizontal to the vertical—the position in which we move through everyday life—shows that the lovers are on the go, able to move in place, swaying as in a dance, or to quickly move apart from one another. One young woman who lived in a walk-up apartment building with her mother reported that she and her boyfriend used to make love in this position in an alcove at the back of the first-floor hallway. The boyfriend was a small-time swindler, and the girl's mother disapproved of the relationship. The lovemaking at the back of the hall reflected the need of both partners to be able to disengage quickly in case anyone came into the hall and also the tenuous, catch-as-catch-can nature of their relationship.

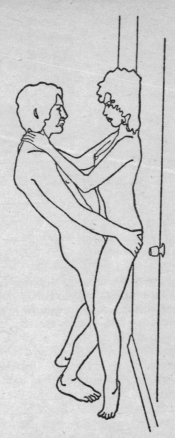

Ten Cents a Dance

The *Trapeze* is a particularly interesting position because of the contradictions inherent in it. It stands as a kind of transition between the missionary and woman-astride positions. The man is seated on a table edge, with the woman on top of him. Yet she leans far back into empty space, as though trying to become horizontal. The man, sitting upright, must bear the

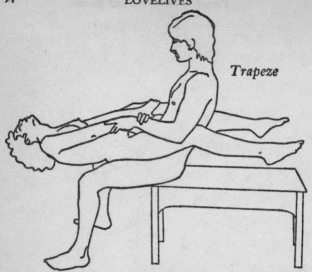

Trapeze

whole weight of the woman as she hangs suspended in midair. The interlocking of the hands and wrists is all that prevents her from falling away from him.

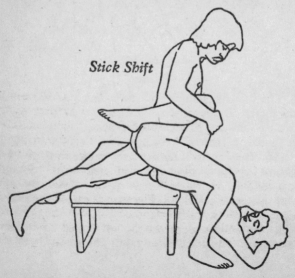

Stick Shift

In the *Stick Shift* position the woman is no longer suspended, but has fallen away from the man altogether. There is resistance in her alignment, while the man manipulates her as though trying to put her into a new position. Although the man is astride, the intimacy that exists in the basic missionary position has been totally disrupted.

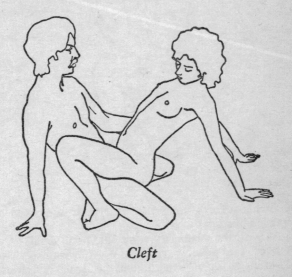

Cleft

The variations on the female-astride position can be numbered in the dozens. This is due in part to the great popularity of such positions in Oriental cultures. It should be remembered, however, that the small, agile bodies of many Oriental peoples facilitate a number of complex positions that might well be uncomfortable or even painful for Western couples. The historical Oriental preference for sitting cross-legged on floor cushions, the widespread practice of Yoga and other philosophical or religious modes of contemplation that involve extensive discipline of the

Sling

body make for a limberness that finds additional expression in sexual activity.

As with the missionary positions, I will detail only a few of the possible variants of the woman-astride position, giving an overview of the significant alternatives in a way that will enable the reader to analyze other similar positions independently. The *Cleft* position shows a certain degree of detachment even though the couple are face to face. The man kneels, leaning backward from the waist with his hand on the bed behind him for support. The woman sits astride him in basically the same position, also with her arms extended behind her. The partners are able to view one another, but there is considerable distance between their heads as they lean backward away from one another. The use of the hands is ruled out because of the need for support, and the emphasis is on the genital component. The fact that the man's torso is lifted off the bed and that both partners assume virtually the same angle of repose in relation to one another makes this one of the less assertive of the astride positions from the woman's point of view. However, since she is above the man, with her weight on his thighs, it is largely up to her to initate and control the movement pattern during intercourse. In spite of the mutual viewing of one another that takes place, this position is contemplative rather than intimate, owing to the absence of manual and facial contact.

It is possible for a couple to move directly from the Cleft position into the more intimate *Sling* position. The man, on his knees, sits straight up, and the woman moves in close to him, her knees half bent, balancing on the balls of her feet while the man places his arms around her buttocks like a sling to give her full support. There is more skin contact in this position, the partner's faces are closer together, and the woman can fondle the man since a hand can be free. He, in turn, is able to use his fingers to stimulate her buttocks. There is considerable equality in this position; both partners are essentially vertical from the waist up, and although the woman is astride the man, he is at the same time using his physical strength to support her with his arms. The woman, however, retains the greater degree of mobility and control over the movement pattern.

Half Shell

The woman appears to be opening the man up in the *Half Shell* position. The man is turned away from her, as though avoiding visual contact. The woman is very active here, while the man passively allows himself to be manipulated. In a more intimate variation on the woman-astride position, the *Wedge*, the woman is trying to get in line with the man, but his raised leg prevents it. She appears almost to be forcing herself upon him.

The *Tugboat* is a position requiring great limberness and agility on the part of the couple and is thus one of the rarer positions. But it is interesting because the woman is astride from the rear, with the man more passive. Both partners view the world from the same perspective but cannot make visual contact with one another. The physical tension necessary to achieving this position reflects a general sense of strain in the relationship.

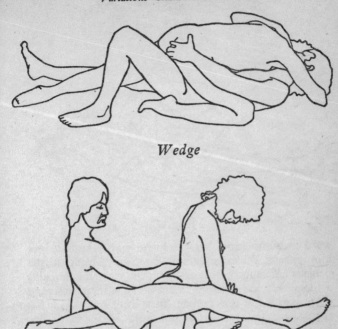

Wedge

Tugboat

In the *Lotus* the man lies supine while the woman sits on top of him, with her back turned to his face, folding her legs into the classic Oriental position of contemplation, with each foot placed on the opposite thigh. The man uses his arms to steady her as she moves above him. Turned away from the man, the woman is like a person meditating upon her own inner world even as she is genitally connected to the man. There is a minimum of physical contact in this position and a maximum of self-absorption on the part of the woman. His hands do support her in her in-

Lotus

ward contemplation, but she in no way acknowledges him except through genital contact. Although the penis is entering the vagina from the rear, this remains a female-astride position because the man is supine, a mere perch for the woman. In a similar position, the *Sidesaddle*, the woman is not only astride with her back to the man, but appears to be about to get up and walk away from him, in a complete show of independence.

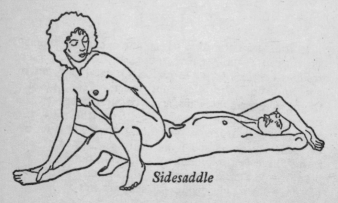

Sidesaddle

In the *Seesaw* position the man is somewhat more active. The woman again is facing away from him, but her feet are placed on the bed or floor. The man, with his arms stretched tautly behind him, lifts his torso and upper legs off the bed to make genital contact. Because of the tension of the man's arched back, extremely deep and close genital pressure can be achieved. The man is free to determine the rhythm to some extent by lifting and withdrawing his body, but the woman, who is almost standing, has the most freedom of relationship here. The basic component of the arched back can be used in several different combinations. The woman can sit facing the man, in which case there is increased intimacy because the partners are facing one another. Or the man may be astride with the woman lifting herself to him, in which case it becomes a variation on the missionary position, with the man having the most freedom in addition to primacy.

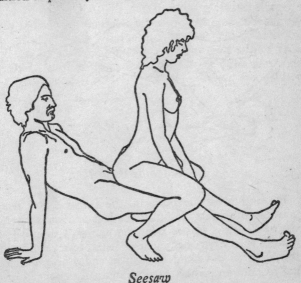

Seesaw

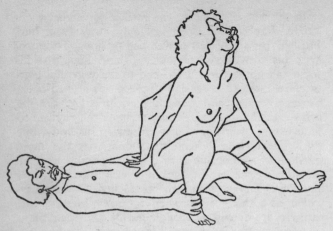

Lover Come Back

Lover Come Back II

In another astride position, the *Lover Come Back* position, the intertwining of the legs and the fact that the man's leg is placed over the woman's shoulder, as though to prevent her escape, delineate a relationship involving an independent woman and a man attempting to hold on to her. A more mutually engaged position, *Lover Come Back II*, shows an even more pronounced intertwining of the legs, with an assertive hanging on by both partners reflected in their interlocked thighs. Even though the partners do not face one another, there is a good deal of close skin contact. The man can be more participatory in this position, holding the woman's breasts or practicing *postillionage*—using his fingers to stimulate her anus. The woman is active here, yet the man is allowed to reach out toward her, to hold her, to touch her body. In spite of the basically supine position of the man, he can contribute to the rhythm of the act by using his upper thigh to apply clitoral pressure, and can exert some degree of control by holding onto her thigh.

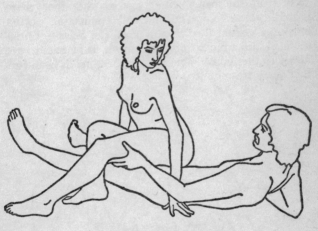

Bon Voyage

However, the *Bon Voyage* position shows the woman drawing away dramatically. Here the man makes no attempt to keep hold of her or to control the situation in any way.

Jackknife

In the *Jackknife* position the woman is folded over away from the man. Neither can see the other, there is minimal skin contact, and full connection occurs only in a genital way. A variation, the *Salaam*, brings the man into a more upright position, as he tries to get closer to the woman—but she, in turn, bends even further away from him.

Salaam

A hassock is used in the *Backbends* position, supporting the man with the woman astride him. They both look upward into distances, but with a wide separation between their respective perspectives. Because the man is supporting the woman, he is penetrating her rather than she riding him. Most strikingly, the partners are heading in opposite directions with only genital contact to keep them together.

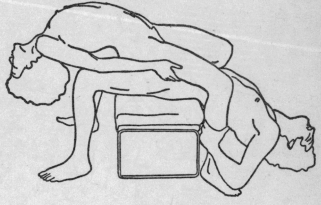

Backbends

In the *Arch* position the man is bent back over a
chair, unable to move and subjugated to the woman's
controlling activity patterns. From the woman's point
of view, this is one of the most dominant of all
woman-astride positions.

Arch

A greater degree of intimacy can be effected in
some woman-astride positions. The *Jockey*, in which
the man is seated in the chair, brings the partners back
into face-to-face contact. Here the woman retains the
flexibility of movement, but the fact the man is sitting
upright, able to look into her eyes, creates a much
greater degree of equality.

It is important to recognize that when a typical

Jockey

woman-astride position is turned in space 90 degrees, so that the man is standing, a very different configuration arises. The man now has his feet planted on the earth, holding the woman around the waist (or under the buttocks) and thus supporting her. In this *Papoose* position the woman clings to the man, trying to merge with him as she wraps her legs around him. There is face-to-face intimacy, but the woman is dependent, and the man shows his strength by grasping her firmly and supporting her. A female patient I treated had a fantasy that she and I would make love in this position. This woman's husband was bisexual and did not offer her the kind of male support she needed. At this same time the woman had a dream in which she was riding a horse and approached a crossroad but did not know which fork to take. In her life she was facing important decisions, and both her dream and her transference fantasy concerning me showed her wish to be carried through to her decisions by a dependent relationship with a strong, supportive male figure.

Papoose

A standing position in which the woman is, in fact, astride is the *Brace*. The man here is inert and relatively fixed in place, while the woman is capable of a great deal of movement. The man can reach around the woman to play with her genitals or anus, but otherwise, he cannot move. A doorway is either an entrance or exit, but the man here is fixed in the door space itself, while only the woman is free either to come or to go.

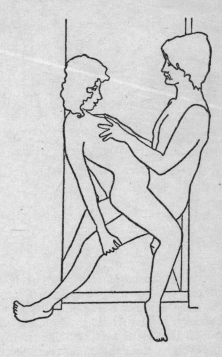

Brace

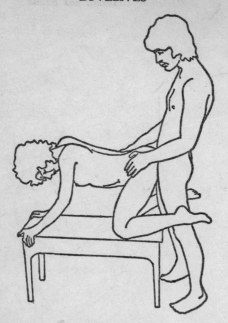

Croupade

In commonly used terminology the square on rear-entry position is known by the French term *Croupade*. The most common variation on this position is called *Cuissade*. Here there is a mingling of thighs as in the frontal Flanquette position. The man is still on top of the woman and penetrating from the rear, but there is greater genital equality. There is much skin contact in this position and the greatest intermingling and intimacy possible in a rear entry position.

A particularly interesting position, phenomenologically, is the *Bobsled*. Here we have a compromise between the assertiveness of the female-astride position and the assertiveness of the rear-entry position. As in all compromises, the dominance is somewhat dissipated on both sides. The woman has more

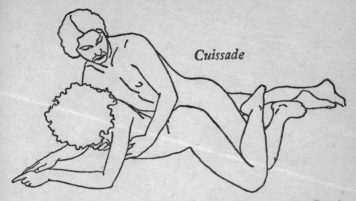

Cuissade

freedom of action, yet the man can help guide genital rhythmic patterns with the strength of his hands and arms. Visually it is possible for the man to participate in the action, while the woman cannot.

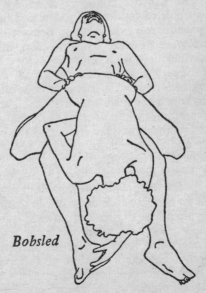

Bobsled

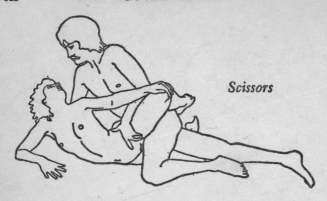

Scissors

The *Scissors* position allows the woman to encircle the man with her legs as he enters from the rear. She thus effects a closeness of lower body contact and establishes greater control than in most rear-entry positions because she has considerable ability to move. The male is able to fondle her breasts and to assist her through masturbatory stimulation. Because the woman can turn toward or away from the man, this position can be emotionally open or closed.

The *T Square* is a rear-entry position with an extreme lack of intimacy. It is almost impossible for the woman to touch the man with her hands, and there is limited visual contact. It is as though the upper portion of the woman's body were out of the picture, existing on a different plane, leaving her to respond emotionally all by herself.

In the *Wheelbarrow* position the woman is being handled by the man. There is minimum physical contact, with an extreme lack of emotional intimacy. The woman's attention is directed toward the floor on which she supports her torso, while the man is necessarily preoccupied with lifting and maneuvering her lower body. The configuration of this position and the physical difficulties involved turn the woman almost into an object to be steered around in life. A

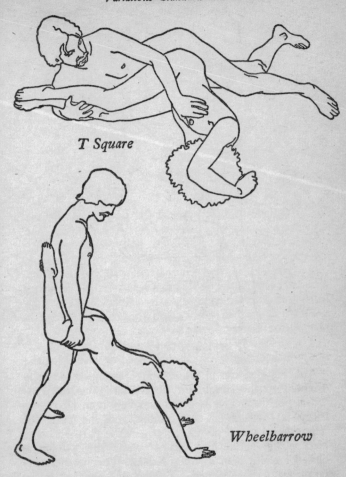

T Square

Wheelbarrow

variation of the Wheelbarrow allows the woman to support herself on a bed or chair. Because the man can place his arm around her middle, and she can look at him there is somewhat more contact and closeness here.

Wheelbarrow Variation

Another position in which much attention must be directed to the simple physical situation is the *Pinwheel* position. This is a position in which all physicality is focused on the genitals and the buttocks. There is no visual contact between the partners. The man is the active participant, while the woman is closed off and bent in upon herself. The partners become even more closed off from one another if the man continues to go forward from the Pinwheel position until his arms are on the floor supporting his torso. Only genital contact remains in this *Somersault* position, in which the two bodies move away from one another like two tumblers who are always flip-flopping apart.

Pinwheel

Somersault

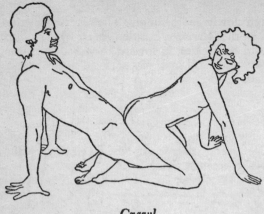

Crawl

The *Crawl* changes the picture somewhat. Here the man is stationary, while the woman is mobile. Again we have a compromise between the woman-astride and rear-entry positions. But there is a distinct sense

Mercury

of the woman's moving away from the man, even though slowly and haltingly. The reverse situation occurs in the *Mercury* position. Here the woman appears to be backing in toward the man, attempting to make contact and lock him to her by raising her leg upward behind his back. The raised thigh invites deep penetration by the man. There is more skin contact than in the usual rear-entry position and a greater degree of mutuality.

A side rear-entry position, the *Twist* allows the man a greater degree of visual contact with the woman. He can see more of her body and it is possible for her to look back at him, creating more intimacy than in most rear-entry positions. A variation, the *Twist II*, makes use of a table, with the man standing behind the woman as she lies on her side. Here, she looks back at him with participatory directness.

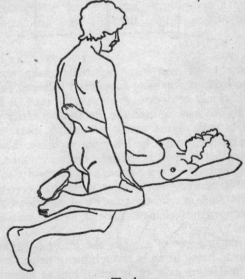

Twist

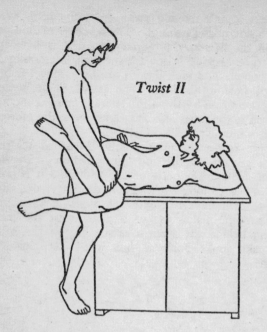

Twist II

A number of rear-entry positions make use of props to aid in maintaining support or balance. Tables, chairs, hassocks or doorways all may be used. A table or a high bed may be used for the *Double Helix* position. The male is the active participant here; with his feet on the ground he has great mobility. The female is curled in upon herself and quite immobile. Yet the intermingling of the partner's legs provides an element of tenderness not always present in rear-entry positions. And, as with the two Twist variations, there is a strong visual element present in this rear-entry position.

Also making use of a table, the *Boost* position has the woman being lifted as though being helped over a fence. She leaves everything up to him as though reluctant to move forward.

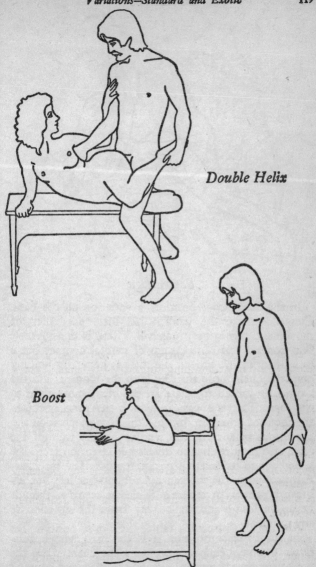

Double Helix

Boost

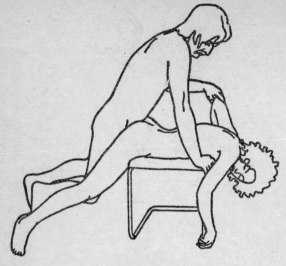

Scrimmage

In the *Scrimmage* position, a variation on the basic Cuissade entry, the woman has little possibility of movement and is very passive. There is considerable skin contact and a maximum of genital contact but a lack of intimacy. Indeed the male is generally holding onto the chair more than he is to the woman, and the woman is forced to relate to the chair more than to the man. This is a case in which the prop becomes the focus of attention. In the *Cliff-Hanger* position the precarious balance of the woman on the edge of the table also requires her to divert her attention from the sexual act to its external circumstances. The man partially supports the woman by holding her leg, but his grasp is somewhat tenuous; it almost seems as though he might let go and walk away from the situation at any moment.

In the *Primate* position it is the man who is relatively passive, being supported by the chair, while the woman pushes backward against the male and controls

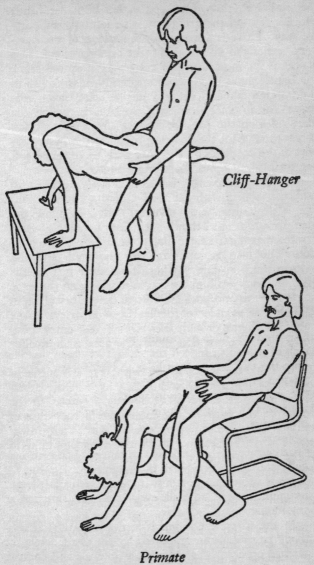

Cliff-Hanger

Primate

the genital rhythm. The woman has both her hands and her feet on the ground in a structurally supportive way. There is a maximum separation of the partner's bodies and no visual contact between them. This is one of the most active of rear-entry positions from the female point of view. Interestingly, it is similar to the position taken in many animal orders. Lower primates, for instance, assume a position in which the male rides on the back of the female's thighs during penetration, with the female providing the basic support as she crouches on all fours with rump raised and her torso in an upward-arching attitude.

A standing rear-entry position, the *Flying Buttress*, finds the woman with her head supported by the wall. She is genitally open, however, and does allow the man to press up behind her. The *Leaning Tower* creates maximum skin contact for a rear-entry position. The man is supported by the wall, and the woman leans on him, yet both have their feet on the ground. They are looking at the world from the same point of view, and both are able to move forward into it. The man is able to fondle the woman while she holds his thighs or buttocks. Of all rear-entry positions, this is the one that shows the greatest mutuality between the partners.

The *Bowknot* is a position with several contradictory elements to it. However, it moves in the direction of the mutuality of side-by-side positions. In the Bowknot, the partners are entangled, in the sense of holding onto one another's waists with their lower legs, and neither partner is clearly dominant in spite of the fact that the woman is essentially astride. Both have some pelvic mobility. But while there is a complete intermingling of the lower part of their bodies, the heads are as far apart as they can be and moving in opposite directions. The position has a certain equality to it, but while there is genital commitment, a strong sexual link, the separation of the heads indicates considerable mental and emotional distance.

Flying Buttress

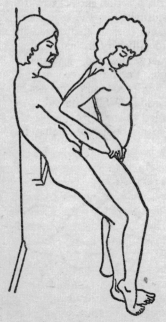

Leaning Tower

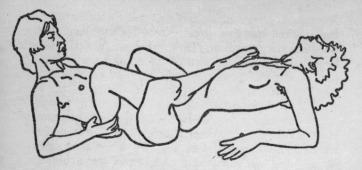

Bowknot

Another position that is marked by lack of face-to-face contact is the *Right Angle*. Both are lying on their sides, with the man between the woman's legs—but at right angles to her. This position moves toward but does not complete the mutuality of the true face-to-face side position. The male patient mentioned in the previous chapter who had difficulty in maintaining an erection in the missionary position, eventually came to use the Right Angle. Yet he arrived at this position only after he had achieved some success in adopting the missionary position. While the side-by-side position had always seemed to me a reasonable alternative in respect to this man's sexual problems, he

Right Angle

was able to discover that fact for himself only after he had worked out to a great extent his problems with the missionary position. Having thus established a sexual self-image that confirmed his confidence in himself, he was able to move on to the side position that was probably most satisfactory for him. Yet it is important to note that he did not adopt a true, full side position involving face-to-face intimacy with his wife. He still had not altogether shaken himself free of his wariness of women and so kept his body at a right angle to his wife's, having a connection, yet avoiding the face-to-face confrontation that caused him anxiety. Another side position, the *Bridge*, brings the partners into closer alignment. The woman's legs are placed over the man as though to hold him more closely to her.

Bridge

To conclude this chapter, let us look at a position that parallels the equality and mutuality of the side-by-side position, but which has a vertical rather than a horizontal configuration. The *Accordion* position achieves maximum face-to-face and eye-to-eye contact. There is mutual embracing, not only with the arms but with the legs as well. This is a position designed for a contemplation, the one of the other, based on equality and mutuality, while at the same time having genital contact. It is a position that requires a certain limberness of the body, just as it reflects a limberness of personality.

Accordion

CHAPTER 7

Other Entry Ports

When partners engage in sex, the love unity that they seek is most completely and most easily established through genital-to-genital contact. Sometimes, however, alternate entry ports are used, either in combination with, in addition to, or instead of the usual mutual genital contact. The use of some of these alternative entry ports is very common; others are more rarely employed. When another entry port is used, it is treated as a genital area. It becomes genitalized, so that the mouth, for instance, is no longer simply a mouth but takes on genital aspects from the point of view of the participants. But since these other entry ports are not as reactive as the sex organs themselves or are reactive in different ways, they cannot always succeed in establishing the love unity. They are not merely physical alternatives, though; some attempt at creating the love unity is always involved.

Let us begin with the most common of these alternative entry ports, the hand. When one partner uses the hand to masturbate the other or both partners do so simultaneously, a very different phenomenological situation exists than that which exists when the contact is between the genitals. The hand is used to handle, to manipulate the world. It is used to order the world, to grasp it, to caress it, to tickle it, to weigh it, and to strike it. When the hand is used to manipulate the genitals of the opposite sex, it is usually the hand itself that is the active agent rather than the penis or vagina that is being manipulated. It is possible for the hand to be passive, with the penis being thrust back and forth through it, or the pelvis raised and lowered so that the vagina moves back and forth over the hand, but this is not ordinarily the case. Usually, in order for stimulation effective enough to cause orgasm to be achieved, the hand must be quite active.

The hand can be cupped so that it becomes a receptacle—a substitute for the vagina. Or the fingers may be used as a substitute for the penis. Because the hand is so flexible, and its touching capacity so minutely localized in a spatial sense, it can touch the exact point that must be stimulated—the clitoris, for instance, or the frenulum of the penis—whereas in actual intercourse there is more generalized contact and stimulation.

It is important to remember that the hand is not a mere instrument, in the way that a mechanical vibrator is, for example. The hand has a tactile sensitivity of its own; it is able to feel what it touches, and there is a feedback through the nervous system to the person who is using the hand. Yet the hand is not capable of orgasm. When the genitals are interlocked in intercourse, both the penis and the vagina are active and reactive at one and the same time. But the hand is primarily active. What is important is what is happening to the genitals it touches, not what happens to the hand itself.

The hand, then, is in a sense detached from what it is doing in a way that the genitals never are. Indeed, the hand may reach out over a considerable distance to touch the genitals, so that the partner whose hand is being utilized may be at a maximum physical distance from the partner who is being manipulated. Thus it is possible for the partners to keep in touch at the extreme of separation. Because the hand is not reactive, it is more bound to ordinary time than the genitals are. During intercourse, as orgasm is approached, the genitals begin to react in a way that transcends time; there is a sudden rush to meet the future, to merge with the universe, that the more objective hand cannot by itself experience. The use of the hand therefore creates a certain distancing between the partners, and only the partner who is being manipulated has the opportunity to experience the transcendence of time that is characteristic of entry into the love world. Sometimes, of course, both partners will manipulate the other simultaneously, but there is still a distance between them that does not exist when the genitals are mutually interactive.

The person who is being manipulated will be gratified by the pinpoint precision of the hand, but without maximum body involvement. From the passive recipient's point of view, there is still a relationship to a person. That is, the hand is attached to a human being. Yet because the sole purpose of the hand is to gratify the person who is receiving the manipulation, there is to some extent a deflection from the twoness of intercourse to a singleness of response. For the person who is utilizing the hand to masturbate the partner, there is to some degree an element of performing a service for the other. The emphasis is not on the interlocking self-gratification and loss of self that occur in true love-sex transcendence, but instead predominantly on the gratification of the partner. To masturbate the partner to climax can be an expression of generosity, giving the partner a helping hand in entering the love world. But there is another side to this coin, in that the act of masturbation may be a way of saying, "I will help you to enter, but I do not wish to accompany you." Obviously the side of the coin that is being exhibited will depend on the circumstances of the act.

When masturbatory techniques are used during the arousal phase, leading on to subsequent intercourse and mutual orgasm, they become simply a matter of initial stimulation and can be very helpful in bringing both partners to the same level of excitement, thus fa-

cilitating eventual joint entry into the love world.
When mutual masturbation to orgasm takes place,
there is an emphasis on the physicality of sex, with
special concentration on the genital sphere. For such
mutual manipulation to be fully efficient, there is
likely to be some separation of the bodies, with loss of
skin contact and a reduction in face-to-face intimacy.

The masturbation of one partner alone often occurs
after the other has already achieved orgasm through
intercourse. Thus a man who loses his erection after
ejaculation may use his hand to help the woman
achieve an orgasm or additional orgasms. Similarly,
the woman may manipulate the man if he has difficulty in ejaculating or wishes to do so a second time.
In these situations, where one or both partners have
already achieved orgasm through intercourse, the use
of the hand becomes a means of holding onto the love
unity for an extended period of time.

Oral sex, the use of the mouth as another entry
port, is also becoming more openly acknowledged. As
has been pointed out before, the experiencing of the
partner through taste means that a part of the partner—the basic molecules of the person—are made a
part of oneself. Although less flexible than the hand,
the mouth is capable of a broader range of activities.
The presence of that extraordinary instrument the
tongue makes possible the creation of a number of
different sensations for the person receiving oral min-
istrations. The genitalized mouth is capable not only
of encompassing but also of probing and penetrating;
it can stroke, lick, nip, and kiss. Because oral sex involves the actual tasting of the partner, there is more
intimacy than with the use of the hand. But the primary focus is on the partner's genitals, rather than the
whole person, so that the love unity is limited.

There are a wide variety of positions possible in
oral sex, a few of which are illustrated here. The same
criteria I have used in analyzing the standard positions

and their common and exotic variations may be used by the reader to arrive at an understanding of oral sex variations. But it should be pointed out that a paradox occurs when the woman practices fellatio, sucking the man's penis. Most men feel that when a woman is sucking them, she is the submissive or passive partner. Yet the man is relatively inactive, standing or lying quite still, while the woman is extremely active, using the mouth and the head and often moving the shoulders back and forth as well. This paradox, in which the inactive partner experiences the sexual act in a way that makes him feel that he is the dominant or even aggressive agent, is probably caused by the combination of several factors. First, there is the somewhat taboo nature of the act itself, making it seem as though the active partner were submitting to the inactive one. Secondly, from a perceptual point of view, the inactive person can watch the active one performing, and thus feel dominant. The existence of this paradox may help explain why many men who cannot

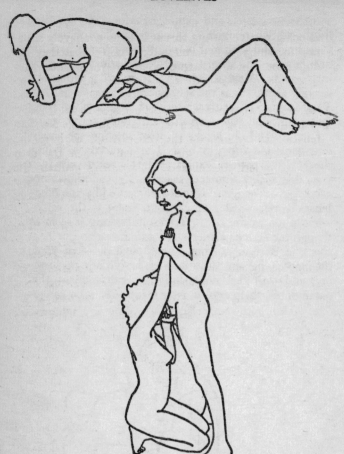

tolerate actual intercourse because of the anxieties it holds for them, are able to respond successfully to fellatio.

The paradox is accentuated by the fact that women who actively enjoy performing fellatio tend to be particularly assertive sexually and do not see themselves as being passive during this act. Thus we have a situation in which both partners tend to feel that they are dominant. This is not true, however, for women who do not much like performing oral sex, and who do so occasionally "as a favor"; at these times they do see themselves as submitting to the man's desires. Some relatively passive women who do not like to perform fellatio are willing, on the other hand, to have the man perform cunnilingus on them. When the man uses his mouth to stimulate the woman's genitals, the woman does not feel that she has to take responsibility for the act in the way that she would if she were sucking the man. This attitude among some women seems to arise from the old stereotyping of women as sexually passive in general.

One female patient reported being tremendously stimulated by a picture she came across accidentally in a magazine. The illustration showed a man sitting on a couch, leaning back; he was holding a woman upside down around the waist, performing cunnilingus on

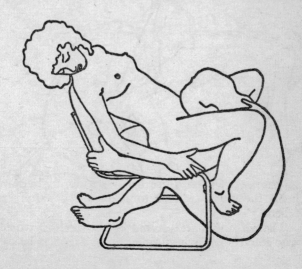

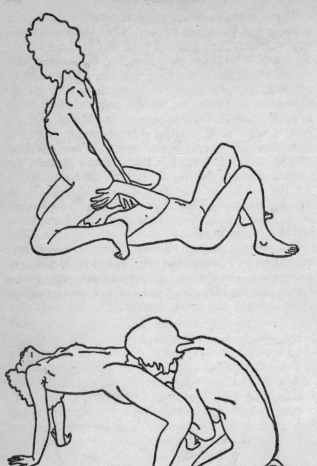

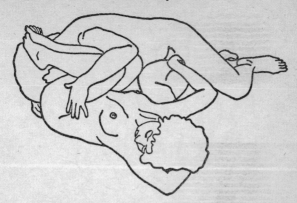

her. My patient associated her excitement with childhood memories of sitting in the lap of her stepfather, who had a seductive attitude toward her. It is interesting to note that in the illustration the woman was not performing oral sex on the man as well, but rather was being held passively by the man.

When oral sex is mutually engaged in, the paradox concerning dominance no longer holds true. In the 69 position both partners tend to feel equally active. The 69 position, especially if it is performed side by side, is experientially a very "democratic" position, with both partners partaking equally of the other. A great deal of skin contact is possible, and the partners may wrap their arms around one another. The fact that they are tasting one another—even swallowing the sperm or vaginal transudate—and the strong element of smell involved compensate to a considerable degree for the loss of face-to-face intimacy. Yet because the mouth is incapable of orgasmic response, this position allows a taste of the love unity but not the full meal.

With anal sex there is contact with the innermost recesses of the body. As with the vagina, and to a lesser extent the mouth, the penis penetrates to a warm central part. The important difference is that

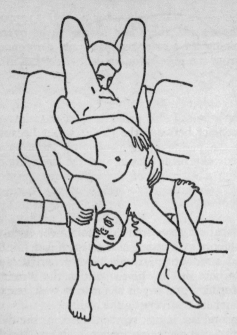

the part here being penetrated is a channel by which feces are eliminated from the body. The penis is reaching toward a part of the body where the life processes are intensely active, as food is converted into metabolic energy. Yet the aspect of this process that the penis actually comes in contact with is the breakdown and decay of matter and its elimination from the body. The feces thus create an element of the taboo. But for some people, the titillation of overcoming the strictures against a forbidden act and penetrating to a secret and vital area may in itself be arousing.

Generally, with anal intercourse, the partner who is being penetrated faces away from the other. Thus we have the aggressive overtones of rear entry, coupled with the use of a taboo entry port. Since the anal sphincter closes reflexively when an object approaches from the outside, there is a barrier to be overcome. Overcoming the barrier requires quite determined activity from the penetrator, as well as relaxation, compliance, and acceptance on the part of the person who is being penetrated. Anal intercourse may take place face to face, although not quite as comfortably as vaginal intercourse. This provides greater intimacy and visual contact between the partners, but because the legs of the person being penetrated must be raised high, generally being placed over the shoulders of the partner in a variation of the missionary position already described, there is still considerable distance between them.

One woman in her thirties has childhood memories of her father lying on the bathroom floor taking enemas. This woman practiced anal masturbation as a child and, when she grew up, had a masturbatory fantasy in which she was given enemas by an intimidating nurse. Later she began to practice anal intercourse with a lover who was quite skilled at this sexual modality. She fondly remembers an episode that brought her consummate pleasure, when her lover, using rear entry, alternated vaginal and anal thrusts without any break in rhythm. It should be noted that because of the stimulation of the pubococcygeal muscle, orgasmic responses can be triggered with anal intercourse even without vaginal penetration.

There are several less commonly employed alternate entry ports. Interfemoral sex involves thrusting the penis between the partner's thighs, from either the front or the rear. The male is usually the more active partner. The penis is close to but separated from the vagina in this position; there is some possibility of stimulation of the vagina through friction without actual penetration. When interfemoral sex is practiced face to face, there is intimate facial contact, but because of the lack of genital contact, the overriding relationship is one of closeness without involvement.

The woman must to some extent have a rigid spatiality in this position, holding her thighs together and not moving the pelvis much if the male is to achieve orgasmic sensation. The limitation on the woman's freedom of movement emphasizes her lack of involvement. While interfemoral sex is sometimes employed to the point of orgasm (in some cases for contraceptive reasons), it is more often used during the arousal phase or as a variation during the plateau phase, with orgasm occuring through actual intercourse.

Intermammillary sex is similar to interfemoral sex. That is, a nongenital area that is not a body cavity is used to create friction against the penis. In this case the squeezing or holding of the penis between the breasts allows a sense of containment since the plasticity of the breasts allows them to be molded to the penis. Because the breasts are an extremely responsive erogenous zone for the woman, she can become quite stimulated by intermammillary sex. This is an extremely visual position for the male, since he can watch the penis moving between the breasts and view the moment of ejaculation. The woman, too, can watch the ejaculation, and the sensation of the warm semen on the chest is arousing to some women. Either the male or the female may mold the breasts to the penis, thus affording the woman a greater sense of participation than in some of the other variations discussed in this chapter. For the man, there is considerable distancing from the female genital area, but for the woman, there is quite intimate contact with the penis, in both a tactile and a visual way.

In gluteal sex the penis is placed in the gluteal fissure, the anal crease between the mounds of the buttocks. If the partners are of the right height, this can be carried out by the male's standing behind the woman with both partners upright. Or it may be done while the man lies beneath the woman. In *Sleep Positions* I described the case of a *frotteur* who preferred to have sex by rubbing his penis against women in this manner. He favored the standing position and was sent to me for treatment after being arrested for molesting women in the subways.

In the case of this patient, friction was achieved through thrusting movements, but it may also be effected through rhythmic contractions of the woman's gluteal muscles or by pelvic rotation on the part of one or both partners. The phenomenological and relationship patterns are self-evident, equivalent to rear entry, except that there is a distancing from the genital center. Gluteal sex may sometimes be used during the arousal stage since there is a strong element of touch gratification involved, for the woman as well as the man.

And among others, there is axillary sex, in which the penis is inserted in the armpit. This is a rare form of sexual activity but one that is sometimes practiced as a result of a male's attachment to a cavity that is wet and has hair but is at some distance from the real genitals. The male may face the female's feet or her head, but in either position visual contact between the partners is lost. The male is usually the active partner, although the woman may use some shoulder movements. Axillary sex is in essence a form of masturbation, but because the armpit lacks the flexibility of the hand, the man must actively thrust in and out of it instead of being manipulated. There is a novelty factor in this situation that may give some titillation to both partners, but because the novelty factor is so extreme, it becomes in itself the focus of the act, undermining the possibilities of transcendence even for the active male.

CHAPTER 8

Rhythm and Release

The positions that have been analyzed in the last three chapters indicate fundamental relationship patterns between partners. Some couples usually limit themselves to one basic position that is physically and psychologically reassuring for the duration of each episode of lovemaking and seldom vary this particular position when they have intercourse. Others may vary positions considerably during a given episode or separate ones. Yet even those couples who experiment a good deal are likely to return to certain positions more often than others. This is particularly true in respect to the orgasmic phase. As the couple approach orgasm, there is an increased need to have a stable reassuring platform from which to launch themselves into the love world. We have seen, for instance, that many couples will utilize one position as one partner reaches orgasm and then switch to another in order to facilitate the climactic striving of the other.

But the positions themselves are not the whole story. There is also the matter of the overall rhythm of the sexual encounter to consider. This rhythm is determined by the kind of movement pattern employed—thrusting, rocking, or grinding movements—and by the pace at which these different kinds of movement proceed. Chinese sex manuals, from ancient times, have placed particular emphasis on the importance of such movement patterns. They differentiate among shallow and deep thrusting, shallow and deep rotating, when a grinding maneuver is used, and shallow and deep side-to-side rocking. Often the Chinese texts recommend special combinations of shallow and deep movement. For example, in a position which the Chinese called the *Dragon in Flight* (which is similar to the Locomotive position outlined in the variations chapter) the male is admonished to create a pattern involving "eight deep and six shallow" thrusts until both partners are "overwhelmed and the *clouds burst.*" In another position, *The Tiger in the Forest* (a rear-entry position), the male alternates five shallow and six deep thrusts for a total of 100. At the end of this period, the manual assures the reader, "the jade flower will be flowing with secretions which will wash away the cares of life." The jade flower, of course, is the vagina. This position was supposed to benefit the heart and the liver, as well as achieve sexual pleasure.

In another position, "Lady Precious Yin and her Lord Yang," as the lovers are called, stand in front of a couch. She places one foot on the couch, and he slowly penetrates her, moving with a rhythm of nine shallow and one deep thrusts until "the Flower Heart is completely open and the Perfume Dew covers it." This position is called the *Standing Bamboos*, but once the "Perfume Dew" has appeared, the bamboos bend before the wind, and orgasm is achieved as the couple lie back on the couch itself. The Standing Bamboos position was credited with banishing hunger and promoting longevity.

The thrusting pattern may also be under control of the woman. For instance, in the *Swinging Monkey* position, the Great Lord Yang seats himself in a chair placed under a low tree in the garden, grasping an overhanging branch. Sitting in his lap, facing him, Lady Precious Yin slides up and down over his penis without allowing it to enter the "inner chamber." When the excitement becomes unbearable for both of them, she fully encompasses the penis and uses nine

deep and five shallow thrusts successively until orgasm
is achieved.

It is significant that these ancient manuals recommend different kinds of rhythms for different positions. In fact, when the various positions are viewed
functionally, some lend themselves to deep thrusting
while others do not. In addition, some positions are far
more congenial to the use of rocking or grinding mo-
tions than are others. Thus, the movement pattern that
is employed and, indeed, the identity of the more active partner will often be influenced by the fundamental position that is selected. Position and rhythm
are thus often closely linked.

The missionary and rear-entry positions, together
with their many variations, are particularly suited to
powerful thrusting by the man. We have seen that
women who are very passive in the missionary position, with their legs extended, allow the man almost
totally to initiate and control the thrusting pattern.
On the other hand, women who raise their legs somewhat, flexing them at the knees and hips, are able to
return the male thrust, the woman lifting and moving
toward the man as he moves against her. In this situation the rhythmic pattern becomes a collaborative
venture; either the woman or the man is free to alter
the pace of intercourse, to slow or quicken the
rhythm. Of all the missionary positions, the Locomotive, where the woman's legs are raised high in the air
across the man's chest and shoulders, gives the male
the greatest leverage for deep and powerful thrusting.
The woman has some ability to return the male thrust,
but her mobility is not nearly as great as his, and this
remains a position in which male control of the
rhythm is extremely pronounced.

A male patient of mine grew up under the domination of a very authoritarian mother, in sibling com-
petition with a sickly elder brother who had always
absorbed his mother's attention. The man early adopted a psychological pattern of defeatism, combined

with a dependence on women. As a young man he was very shy and unable to approach women, but eventually he married a rejecting and repressed woman. The marriage broke up when he sought to build up his self-image through an extramarital affair. He now has a good relationship with a sexually responsive woman, but their sexual pattern reflects both his passivity and his need to break out of it. He states that the woman usually has a few orgasms in the astride position, during which she controls the movement. But he then swings her into a missionary position and thrusts strongly as he approaches his own orgasm. He describes this thrusting by saying that it is as though his penis were a pistol that he is striving to drive through the posterior wall of the vagina. At this point he feels himself to be a man and at the same time expresses his attempt to "break through" to communication with women in general.

When the woman is astride, of course, she tends to control the movement pattern. Some women report that they enjoy sliding up and down the erect penis; here the woman thrusts herself *upon* the man. But the woman-astride positions also lend themselves to grinding and rocking movements. The woman may rock her body from side to side so that the man's penis is in particularly close contact with first one side and then the other side of the vagina. Grinding movements, in which the woman rotates herself on the penis, are most easily carried out in the positions in which the woman's pelvis, legs and thighs have the greatest freedom. Thus the Lotus position is especially suited to such swiveling of the woman's body, since her legs are in no way contained by the male.

In the woman-astride position the woman may use the male organ essentially as a fulcrum upon which she moves. Some men find that when the woman is astride and using either a grinding or a rocking motion, the stimulus to the penis is more subtle and the pressure on it less intense than when they are thrusting; for this reason it is sometimes possible for the man to prolong intercourse and put off orgasm more successfully when the woman controls the movement pattern. At the same time, of course, they are demonstrating a certain passivity in relinquishing control. For many of these men, however, it is necessary to reassert a degree of initiative when they do wish to ejaculate, by either thrusting from below the woman or turning into another position in which the thrusting movement can be more strongly pressed.

One patient, a man in his thirties, had difficulties in expressing his feelings and in committing himself in relationships. These emotional inhibitions carried over into his sexual life. He had difficulties in achieving and maintaining an erection and was prone to premature ejaculation. Because the position protected him from having an orgasm too quickly, he preferred to have the woman on top. He had formed a relationship with a woman who was unable to have orgasms at all because of strong sexual repression. The fact that she had never had an orgasm with any man lifted the responsibility for her pleasure from him, and he found that with her he was less likely to have a premature ejaculation. Despite the woman's sexual repression, she was able to take the astride position with this man because of his extreme passivity.

In most cases where couples seem to be mismatched sexually, the ensuing struggle between them may be to achieve dominance. Yet sometimes there is a struggle to retain the greater passivity. In one such case a male patient was married to a very detached woman. The wife insisted on having sex in the rear-entry position, as might be expected of a woman who had difficulty in making an emotional commitment to a man. But the husband was a very passive individual; predictably he did not like the rear-entry position, which is the most aggressive of male positions. Not only did this position impose on him the need to express an assertiveness he did not feel, but it also disturbed him because his wife seemed unwilling to move toward him and be open with him. Although he saw his wife as the dominant personality, in their sexual relations he found himself placed in the position of having to control the rhythm of the encounter. The particularly deep thrusting possible in the rear-entry position was alien to his diffident nature.

In regard to the initiation and control of the pace and rhythm of intercourse, my patients and other individuals appear to fall into three separate groups. First, there is an assertive type, individuals who feel a strong need to dominate the sexual situation in terms of both position and ongoing activity. The assertive type may be either a male or a female, but there are a greater number of males in this group. Many males, accepting the stereotyping of the role of the male as sexually dominant in our society, believe that they *should* be assertive and so do their best to fulfill the cultural self-image they have been taught. In the Kinsey studies it was shown that upper-class couples would assume the female-astride position far more often than working-class couples. At the time of the Kinsey surveys in the late 1940's and early 1950's working-class males considered the more passive "man on the bottom" position as a threat to their masculine image, while the more sophisticated upper-class males were less likely to be bound by this inhibition. Although there have been no subsequent studies of the scope of Kinsey's work, a number of recent reports indicate that there is now a greater acceptance of the female-astride position among blue-collar workers. Yet there remain a great many men who feel that they should regulate the sexual encounter and who feel uncomfortable and even anxious if they are not allowed to do so.

A second type is generally complaisant in the sexual arena, as they are in their lives in general. These men and women prefer to have their partners establish

position and rhythm, taking charge of the situation.
Such individuals will accommodate—a word they often use—themselves to the partner's pattern of movement and rhythmic pace. Some men who pride
themselves on being "good lovers" say that they accommodate themselves to the woman, taking their
cues from her and doing their best to give her
pleasure. One patient is married to a woman who is
very repressed, and the relationship between them is
difficult, unemotional, and cold; with her he uses the
missionary position and sets the rhythm. But with
other women he likes to have the woman astride and
likes to watch them enjoying sex. He will set the initial movement pattern with them, but during the
plateau phase he allows the woman to take charge,
telling him to "do this or don't do that." He defers to
the woman's likes and states that "her enjoyment is
the best part for me." He cannot get an erection with
prostitutes, however; they automatically put him off
because they don't mean what they say, their responses aren't genuine, and he can't trust them.

Another man who enjoys "turning women on" is a
well-known rock entertainer. His bed is surrounded
by mirrors—he must see himself as a star performer
even in his sexual life. Yet the obvious narcissism involved here is balanced by a need to have "audience
response." He wants to be able to see the woman respond with excitement and pleasure to him. This man
practices karezza—withholding ejaculation—so that he
can continue to bring the woman to orgasm over a
longer period of time. Sometimes he himself experiences orgasm but without emission. Although he uses
the missionary position, the need to be face to face
with his audience of one is as important as the dominance of the configuration. He accommodates himself
to the woman in the sense that her orgasm is more important than his, yet at the same time it is important
for him to be in control of *himself*, avoiding ejaculation, so as to have the stamina left to urge the woman

on to greater excitement. In other words, he dominates by giving pleasure and is thus a mixture of types.

The third major type of individual places the greatest importance on the mutuality of the encounter. In relationships between two such partners there is a great deal of give-and-take, first one and then the other setting the pace and choosing the movement pattern. Such couples may show some preference for a side-by-side position, in which each has equal freedom of movement, or for the Accordion position described at the end of Chapter Six, where equality and mutuality are also emphasized. But such couples are likely to be particularly experimental, in a very genuine way, switching positions several times during intercourse, handing back and forth to one another the sexual reins. Cooperative couples tend to have a rich personal relationship in many aspects of their life together, and this will be reflected in the variety of their sexual repertoire.

As partners approach the orgasmic phase, and the intensity and pace of the movement increase, bodily communication becomes more finely attuned. The signals that partners give to one another indicating the onset of orgasm vary greatly. Many of those signals may be in the form of vocal utterances, either verbal or nonverbal; these will be explored in the next chapter, "Love Songs." Physical signals always involve patterns of reaching or holding—and sometimes both at once. Arms and legs may be extended to their utmost as the person reaches out to infinity. An individual may clasp the partner with great strength in order to carry the other with them into the final ecstasy or to be carried by them. Involuntary body spasms are very common. The coordination and control that have been exercised during the arousal and plateau phases are all at once abandoned, and the whole body lets go. Individuals who have at one time or another experi-

enced orgasm under circumstances where it was
necessary to prevent other people from realizing that
sexual intercourse was taking place—like the young
woman who made love with her boyfriend standing at
the back of the hallway—have commented on the
great strain involved in not completely letting go, in
trying to control the orgasmic reaction so as not to
make too much noise or attract attention. The intensity of the orgasm lies exactly in the fact that control
is lost; one abandons oneself completely to the spasm
of pleasure. When that abandoning cannot be fully
experienced, when the individual tries to keep a hold
on the surrounding environment, a contradiction is in-
troduced that causes both a physical and an emotional
straining. Like a "controlled" nuclear reaction, a controlled orgasm can take place only under great
pressure—it goes against nature.

The male orgasm, in fact, cannot be interrupted.
Once prostatic and urethral contractions begin, the
point of no return is reached, bringing orgasmic inevitability. Thus, males who practice karezza, avoiding
ejaculation, must seek to prevent these contractions
from happening. Once they have begun, the contractions occur at intervals of about eight-tenths of a second, strongly at first but then becoming weaker,
irregular, and less frequent.

The female orgasm may be interrupted at any point
in the cycle, but it may also begin again. Actual pelvic
contractions take place, inducing a feeling that is variously described. Some women say that they feel as
though they were falling, other speak in terms of an
opening up, and some feel as though they were emit-
ting fluid. For many women, a sensation of warmth
spreads throughout the body, culminating in a throb-
bing sensation in the pelvis. During masturbation the
average woman takes a little less than four minutes to
reach orgasm, but during coitus some women may
reach orgasm in as little as fifteen to thirty seconds.

Such quick orgasms are usually of the squeak type and may continue for some time.

One of the major debates in the field of sexology over the past few decades has revolved around the problem of premature ejaculation in the male and inability to reach orgasm in the female. The debate, indeed, is not over. A university symposium at Stony Brook, New York, in 1974 dealt extensively with this question. To begin with, what does "premature" mean? According to the Masters and Johnson definition, the male should be able to continue coitus until the female achieves orgasm in 50 percent of the encounters. This definition seems to make the female partner's orgasmic competence the crux of the matter. A male-based definition, offered by Dr. Donald Hastings, suggests that a premature ejaculator is a man who cannot continue in coitus as long as he wants to. But here we run into a problem that complicates definitions of both male and female orgasmic competence. What, for instance, if the male would like to continue for an hour but can last only forty minutes? Surely he is not a premature ejaculator. Yet a case was cited in which a woman complained that her husband was "premature" because he could not last longer than forty minutes. In many cases, of course, it is not a physical or sexual problem but a matter of excessive expectations. It was pointed out that some young college women, for instance, are often distressed that they have only one orgasm instead of a series, not knowing that only sixteen percent of women usually have copulatory multiple orgasms.

So the question arises: After how many minutes of intercourse does a male's ejaculation cease to be premature and become a matter of unrealistic expectations? At the Stony Brook symposium it was suggested that increasing duration beyond a reasonable period does not, in fact, increase the possibility of a woman's achieving orgasm. A rough rule of thumb was stated: If a man can engage in unrestrained fore-play for ten minutes, followed by four to six minutes of vigorous intercourse, it is unlikely that longer peri-ods of time will increase the woman's potential for in-tercourse. This seems a fairly sensible definition, but there are no doubt those who will dispute it, continu-ing the debate.

Most couples strive to have the woman achieve or-gasm first, if it cannot be experienced simultaneously. Some of my patients report that they very often achieve simultaneous orgasm with their regular part-ners, particularly when the sexual pattern is a basically cooperative one. But many other individuals seldom achieve simultaneous orgasm with the partner, and *many do not want to*. I have already presented a num-ber of cases in which the woman will achieve orgasm in one position, with a change of position taking place before the man has his orgasm. Obviously, if two partners achieve orgasm most easily and enter the love world most completely in different positions, mutually successful sex will necessarily involve separate points of orgasmic release.

In some cases the couple will prefer to have the man reach orgasm first. One woman, for instance, says, "I come after the man comes. The penis is softer then, and it touches me in a nicer way." This woman has a very warm and tender relationship with her partner, and she sees sex as an "instant" in the midst of an infinity of love. For her, the emotional aspects of the relationship are paramount: thus, when the part-ner's penis softens after his orgasm, it is clearly easier for her to concentrate on the emotions she feels rather than on the physicality of intercourse. And it is those feelings that carry her to orgasm and allow her to en-ter the transcendent realm of love.

Thus, just as there is no position that is "more nor-mal" than another, so there is no movement pattern or timing of orgasm that is better. There is no set pattern of sexuality that will afford more pleasure than another to everyone; rather, there are specific individual patterns that afford the most pleasure and fulfillment to particular people.

Once orgasm has been achieved, the couple enter the resolution phase of coitus. Without orgasm, of course, there can be no resolution. Not only will the love unity be unachieved, but physical discomfort may exist. Just as men who have been left unsatisfied suffer from prostatic engorgement and pain, so women who have not been satisfied will also experience pain and congestion in the pelvic area. There is a very large number of blood vessels in the female pelvis, a fact that is sometimes advanced as a reason for the longer arousal period required by many women. These blood vessels dilate during intercourse, and their abundance may also affect the longer time needed for full resolution in women.

Aside from physical factors, there is a wide range of emotions that are experienced during the resolution phase, as the partners return from the intensity of the love world to the plane of daily existence. Perhaps the most famous statement concerning this period is attributed to Galen (A.D. 130–200): "Every animal is sad after coitus except the human female and the rooster." But in fact, the feelings that both men and women report having experienced during this phase run the gamut from exhilaration to depression. Probably the most common feeling is one of satiated relief—generally of a physical nature, but occasionally more psychological than physical. A feeling of sadness *is* often felt by women as well as men in spite of Galen's comments. Usually this sadness is an expression of sorrow that the experience is over and that the hold on the love world must be relinquished so quickly.

Disappointment may be felt in response to dissatisfaction with some aspect of the performance or of the relationship. Guilt is a common post-coital feeling, often showing itself in a rejection of the partner or a need to leave the partner immediately. Sexual encounters with casual pickups or extramarital sex often engender guilt. Contempt, hostility, or a sense of power may be felt. These feelings, as well as all the others mentioned here, occur to some degree at various times in all people.

If the sexual experience has been transient or limited in some way, the absence of the love unity may bring a feeling of depression, a feeling of separation, a need to deny the experience, or a flight from it. But these anxieties or defenses against anxiety will not be felt or brought into play by individuals who are unthreatened by the elements of the particular love experience. The couple who have achieved the love unity will, of course, continue to bask in its warming glow throughout the resolution phase.

CHAPTER 9

Love Songs

The sounds—or lack of them—that human beings utter during sexual intercourse tend to reflect, like their sex positions and habits, these individuals' overall ways of living in the world. These sounds may be divided into two major categories: First, there is actual verbalization, the speaking of specific words; secondly, there is vocalization, the uttering of wordless sounds.

The verbalizations may be subdivided into three types: (1) coprophemic or "dirty" words; (2) expressions of endearment, like "I love you"; and, (3) measures of guidance, such as "Quickly, quickly" or "Now, now." Some individuals make use of all these types; others, of none. What is more, these various kinds of verbalization tend to be employed during different phases of the sexual cycle for very different purposes.

It is interesting to note that in any given language there are only a few specifically dirty words. And in most languages they are short words, particularly suitable as expletives. In American English the basic list of dirty words includes "ass," "balls," "cock," "prick," "cunt," "pussy," "twat," "fuck," "piss," and "shit." There are a few words of more than one syllable that are not really sexual in connotation, such as "asshole" and "bastard." There are also certain technical or scientific words, such as "fellatio," "cunnilingus," and "masturbation," which some people consider "dirty." Finally, certain common English verbs become obscene only when used in a sexually connotative way—among these are "to lick," "to suck," "to brown," "to come," and "to ball."

The fact that each culture designates only a few words as taboo paradoxically demonstrates the importance to human beings of such words. If there were too many of them, they would become less powerful. As with pornographic materials, men have in the past made more use of and appeared to be more stimulated by dirty words than women. Once again this seems to show the influence of cultural conditioning and has been changing in recent years. Nevertheless, for most people the taboo words continue to be more shocking when uttered by a woman. Women sometimes suggest that the male fascination with dirty words is a kind of childishness. One of the more eloquent statements of this idea was made a number of years ago by Lady Attlee in her first parliamentary speech after becoming a member of the British House of Lords. The speech concerned the Wolfenden Act, which removed criminal penalties from homosexual acts. Many of the lords had expressed their "disgust" at the very thought of practicing homosexual acts; chiding her male colleagues, Lady Attlee stated that no woman who had been through the experience of childbirth could or should find any function of the human body disgusting.

The use of dirty words during sex is usually limited to the arousal and plateau phases. For partners who do not know one another well, the use of the phrase "Let's fuck" is a way of distancing the act of sex from emotional involvement. If the person using this phrase is uncertain whether the other individual wants to have sex, these bald words make clear that a challenge, rather than a plea, is being uttered and thus make it easier to accept a possible refusal. On the other hand, the occasional use of these words between long-term partners can be a way of reintroducing a sense of excitement into an expected sexual episode.

During the plateau phase the use of dirty words usually indicates a need on the part of the person uttering them for additional stimulation, a spur to further excitement. Those who chronically use such expletives, however, are likely to have a different purpose, using the words to distance the self emotionally from the sexual act in much the same way as a fetishist uses objects.

Expressions of endearment are at the opposite end of the spectrum from the coprophemic words. Interestingly, just as some people have great difficulty in saying a dirty word, others find it difficult to express endearments. But while the inability to say a dirty word may indicate inhibitions concerning the physicality of sex, the inability to express endearments shows a fear of intimacy and commitment.

Endearments are commonly used during the arousal phase, the plateau phase, and the resolution phase. For reasons that will shortly become apparent, both endearments and other specific words are less likely to be used during the orgasmic phase. In general, women appear to regard expressions of endearment as more important than men do, particularly during the resolution phase. The resolution phase is physically of longer duration in women than it is in men. Once the man has ejaculated, his sexual drive in most cases rapidly declines, and a pause is necessary before he can become aroused once again. Many women, however, remain sexually excited for some minutes after orgasm has occurred. During this extended resolution period many women find it particularly important to be held, caressed, and talked to. In troubled marriages a common complaint of the wives is that as soon as their husbands have had an orgasm, they just "roll over and go to sleep"; significantly, the same women often state that their husbands never say, "I love you," and seem to find it difficult to utter endearments in general. Even among men who do express endearments, they may often be couched in physical rather than emotional terms. Thus, instead of "I love you," the man will say, "You're gorgeous," "You're beautiful," or "That was terrific."

It is common for endearments to take the form of diminutives—a kind of baby talk. Is this a sign of regression? I don't believe so. Rather, it seems to be an attempt to regain the directness of experience that we enjoyed as children and to express things without shame or the fear of being censured by "grown-up" standards of conduct. Some feminists in recent years have taken umbrage at the use of words like "baby" and "honey," seeing them as a kind of put-down, intended to keep women aware of their historical dependency. While this may sometimes be true, such words can also be a way of indicating emotional closeness, not superiority.

Words of guidance are most often expressed during the plateau phase, especially as one or both partners approach the verge of orgasm. But partners involved in a long-term sexual relationship are less likely to use words of guidance for the simple reason that they don't need to. Two people with considerable experience of one another's bodily reactions do not need language to communicate their physical needs or the level of excitement that has been reached. Words will be necessary only if one partner wishes to do something quite different or out of the ordinary or if orgasm is for some reason upon the point of occurring much sooner than usual.

Some people use words as release mechanisms when at the point of orgasm or during orgasm itself. A man may cry out, "I'm coming," even though his partner is perfectly aware of the fact from his physical responses. One patient of mine reports that at the midpoint of her orgasm she will say, "Don't stop." Such utterances are not usually a form of communication with the partner but an intensely private cry that is used to help achieve the final breakthrough into the love world. Thus the young woman who cried,

"Don't stop," was not doing so because her partner was withdrawing from her; rather, she was in a sense urging the feeling of transcendence she felt to remain with her as long as possible. It is interesting to note that when sexually aroused, stutterers lose their speech impediments—clearly because they are transcending the daily world in which their vocal inhibitions hold sway.

Two words that are on the borderline between being verbal and nonverbal utterances should be mentioned. The word "no," with the "o" vowel greatly extended, is sometimes used and can be misinterpreted. It is not a command to stop but exactly the opposite, the expression of a desire to maintain something that is about to be torn away. The word "oh," on the other hand, involves a continuing, insistent rise that does not quite break through to completion.

People who cry out, "Oh, God," or, "Jesus Christ," at the point of orgasm are not in any way uttering blasphemy. Again, the implications are quite "otherwise." Such religiously connected words demonstrate the otherworldliness that is associated with the love transcendence. In Japan and other Oriental cultures the moment of orgasm is sometimes referred to as the juncture at which human beings are closest to the gods and most fully in touch with the divine spirit.

Many people do not utter words at all during orgasm but merely vocalize. In this second major category of "love songs" are nonverbal utterances such as moans and whimpers, soft tremulous cries, grunts, groans, quiet screams, loud screams, and sobs. These various nonverbal sounds parallel the physical and emotional state of the person uttering them. Thus the tremulousness of the whimper reflects the tender shaking of the person's whole being that is taking place, a quivering attempt to hold on. Moans are low-grade sounds, a background hum that is pervasive but not intense. A moan does not have a climax and therefore is not bound by time; it can continue indefinitely. The sudden vocal push of the grunt reflects effort, a total concentration of the being over a short period of time in order to overcome or reach something. A groan is a moan that is cut off and communicates a sense that the intensity of the experience almost cannot be borne.

The louder sounds are likely to be uttered by individuals who are quite demonstrative sexually and in their ordinary lives. They are not afraid to be overheard, to have it known that they are in the throes of sexual ecstasy. A shout is the hallmark of sudden tremendous release. A scream, which is produced when air is pressed through tightly tensed vocal cords, rises in a crescendo, reflecting the straining toward breakthrough as the person reaches the state of transcendence. The attempt to achieve the level of discharge, to go beyond the limiting tensions of the body, is expressed in these loud cries. Nonverbal sounds are not patterned and follow no formal linguistic structure; rather, they reflect the basic richness of the primal experience of the love situation.

Many people report that they cannot control such vocal counterpoints to their physical and emotional states and are sometimes unaware of uttering them. Others are able to control them but are aware of a lessening of the richness of the sexual experience when they do so. One man states that when he and his wife have houseguests, he makes an effort to restrain the loud cries he usually lets forth at orgasm, but that when he does this, the sexual experience seems less fulfilling and complete. Clearly, for him, it is important to give vent to his feelings of ecstasy in a vocal way if he is fully to experience the love world; the awareness that other people may be listening violates the sense of privacy he needs to let himself go completely. A patient of mine, a young woman, has an opposite response. When she is in her own apartment, located in a modern building with thin walls, she does not vocalize during sex for fear that her neighbors will hear her. But when she has intercourse in her boyfriend's apartment, where the occupants of the other apartments are strangers to her, she says that she moans loudly.

A young male patient of mine took a small apartment in a residential hotel when he was a university undergraduate. He led an isolated existence, having no real friends, and was without any sexual experience whatsoever. He found that he could clearly hear the sounds of love made by the young couple in the rooms above his, particularly the screams and verbalizations of the woman at orgasm. Night after night he heard these sounds, and they disturbed him deeply. He attempted to shield himself from the sexual stimulation these sounds caused in him by wearing the earphones from his stereo set to bed. But even these were not sufficient to drown out the penetrating sounds of ecstasy from above. Each night he was torn between arousal and dread. Eventually he developed an acute anxiety episode and had himself hospitalized to escape the sounds and the panic they created in him. Unfortunately his picture of a mental institution was greatly at variance with reality, and he discovered that far from being in a sanctuary, he was in a locked ward, filled with the disturbed vocalizations of the other inmates.

One twenty-five-year-old man had a very different reaction to the sounds of love. Also a student, he was studying abroad for a year, cut off from his friends and the girl he planned to marry on returning to the United States. He lived in a tiny, depressing room in a cheap Paris hotel. The room next to his, a double, changed occupants often but was usually taken by young tourists. He did not find the sounds of love filtering through the thin walls disturbing but comforting and would often masturbate when he heard couples making love. The sounds through the walls made him feel less cut off and aided his fantasies about his fiancée at home.

When one partner likes to make vocal sounds during sex and the other does not, it can sometimes lead to difficulties. One female patient of mine reported that her vocalizations deeply embarrassed a man she was having an affair with. Such discrepancies in the ways that two individuals enter the love world can lead to the breaking off of a relationship. If the person who vocalizes tries to control the sounds, the love experience itself becomes limited, but if the sounds are not controlled, the embarrassed partner, who needs silence, is distracted from the achievement of transcendence.

On the other hand, it sometimes happens that a person who vocalizes during intercourse feels that the silent partner is not enjoying the experience, is not "with them," as it were. This, of course, is not necessarily the case. The silent partner may be having an experience of the love world just as ecstatic as the "noisy" one and may enjoy the sounds made by the other without feeling the need to utter a sound.

Among those who do vocalize, the reasons for it and the timing may be quite different. One male patient moans from pleasure throughout intercourse, while a woman patient does not make a sound during intercourse itself but afterward whimpers from the sense of exhaustion brought on by orgasm. Another female patient reports that she utters small cries from the beginning of the plateau phase. Interestingly, this woman has multiple small orgasms of the squeak type that continue throughout the sexual episode. In general, it can be said that among those who do make sounds, men and women who make them throughout intercourse are probably able to enter earlier and more easily into the love world, although this is not to indicate that their experience of the love world is more profound than that of the person who cries out only at the point of orgasm. Both individuals have achieved love's transcendence in the particular way that gives them the greatest sense of fulfillment.

CHAPTER 10

Love Machines and Love Potions

When the way to the love experience is blocked, individuals may find it necessary to use certain sexual detours in order to find a passageway into the love world. One of the more common of such detours is fetishism. The fetishistic object—whether it is a shoe, a stocking, underwear, or a glove—creates a distancing of the individual from the genital center of love. The emphasis is no longer directly on the partner but rather on a part of the partner—not a natural part but an artificial one. The fetish draws the attention away from the genitals themselves and fixes it instead on a peripheral object. This peripheralization shows itself in the fact that many fetishes are objects that are worn on the extremities of the body—gloves, stockings, and shoes. Underwear is, of course, more closely connected with the genitals, but significantly it is used to cover them up. Most fetishistic objects share the quality of being a cover for one part or another of the human body. Moreover, many of them are made of fur or leather, taken from the skins—the external coverings—of animals. Objects chosen as fetishes are sometimes red—an emotional color—but more often are black. A neutral color, black causes an additional flattening out of genitalization.

Because the fetishist fears intimate contact with the genitals and finds it difficult to deal with the physicality of the sexual experience, the chosen object allows for sexual arousal without concentrating on the genital area of the partner. There is a strong element of intellectualization in fetishism—once again a removal of the sex experience from the physical to the mental plane. The objects are sometimes used in conjunction with masturbation, making it possible for the fetishist to enter a fantasy world. But usually the fetishist will request that the partner wear the shoes or gloves during sexual intercourse. There is a paradox here, of course: The objects serve to distance the person from the sexual act, but that distancing in turn makes it possible for the person to engage in sex without fear, thus facilitating direct entry into the love world.

In the past it was believed that fetishists were almost universally male, but recent studies have shown the existence of fetishism among women, too. A distinction should be made between the true fetishist, who always or usually requires the fetishistic object in order to achieve sexual fulfillment, and the occasional use of such objects by individuals who do not need their presence but find that they simply add a little excitement. Thus the man who buys his wife a red lace slip for her birthday and asks her to keep it on while he makes love with her is indulging in mildly fetishistic behavior for the purposes of variety rather than need, and such occasional inventiveness may add piquancy to the pleasures of love.

Fetishism is in some ways related to the instrumentalization and invention utilized in sadomasochistic practices. Those involved in sadomasochism always attempt to construct a fantasy or storybook situation—frequently involving chains, whips, ropes, and bondage—in order to initiate sexual arousal. However, in most cases such practices do not really accomplish that end. In her recent study of sexuality Rosemarie Santini claims that the male sadists she interviewed were usually impotent. She states that there was little actual sexual activity reported as occurring during S&M encounters and that the acting out of the fantasy situation appeared to be more important than sexual release. Clearly, then, the way into the love world has become so thoroughly blocked for many sadists that even the extreme trappings of the S&M experience are not sufficient to stimulate sexual arousal.

The sadist, the masochist, and the true fetishist practice extreme variations on the sexual theme. But the occasional use of mechanical devices for sexual stimulation is as old as history and has been a relatively common occurrence in innumerable societies. As Mantegazza wrote in the late ninteenth century: "Man, not content with the natural pleasure of the sexual embrace, has endeavored to increase it with many and varied artifices, in which his imagination has outdone itself." But these devices are not used merely to increase erotic pleasure; often they serve a psychological function as well, acting as necessary portals into the love world. Sometimes they are used as substitutes for close natural contact, while at other times they are used in addition to such contact. When most couples use these artifices, the objective is to increase pleasure through an emphasis on the physical elements, such as touch, pressure, and the temperature qualities related to touch. Visual elements of shape and color are also sometimes involved.

The devices chosen show a definite relationship to the cultural and technological level of the society in which they are used. Thus in Stone Age societies we find artificial phalli crudely carved from rock, while in our own society we have sleek plastic vibrators powered by electricity. The artificial phallus, or dildo, is in fact the most common sexual device throughout history. Ancient sculptured figures from both Babylonia and India show dildos in the hands of women. The use of dildos in ancient Greece is clearly indicated by references in the works of Aristophanes, and a description of their masturbatory usage appears in the Sixth Mimiamb of Herondas. The Greek dildos, used primarily by women of the middle classes, were of a fairly sophisticated design, constructed of leather and so contrived as to be capable of erection through mechanical means. In the English language the first use of the term "dildo" to describe an artificial phallus occurs in the sixteenth century, cropping up in the works of Ben Jonson, Shakespeare, and others. The word goes back farther than that, but in its earlier meaning it was used as a term to disparage a man sexually. Thus, it could be said that a dildo, in its meaning as an artificial phallus, was better than a dildo, meaning a man who was sexually incompetent.

The electric vibrators of our own time are popular with both women and men. There are two types of vibrator: One has the shape of an artificial phallus, while the other is simply a rapidly oscillating knob or disk. These apparatuses are often used under the prescription of sex therapists to hasten orgasm or even to stimulate the ability to have an orgasm. Such usage is primarily for women. But men also use vibrators in conjunction with foreplay or actual intercourse. For men they can be used to stimulate the penis or other areas of the body through friction and can be employed to facilitate erection by being pressed against the perineum. Both sexes sometimes use vibrators in the anus to create additional stimulus during intercourse.

While vibrators are often used for masturbation, we are more concerned here with their effect on intercourse between partners. Because a vibrator is a mechanical device, it obviously may be employed for its distancing effect, detaching the individual from close contact when there is fear of intimacy or immediate physical contact. On the other hand, the device can serve to bring the couple closer together when it is used to overcome inhibition or to create additional mutual stimulation between partners who are sexually open with one another to begin with.

Another device, the penile ring, may be used to stimulate both partners even though it is worn by the man. Such rings also have a very ancient history. Variations on them are to be found in many primitive cultures, and jade rings for this purpose survive from ancient China. The simple penile ring, sometimes worn around the shaft of the penis but often large enough to encompass the testicles, assists in achieving an erection and prevents too rapid detumescence, thereby prolonging pleasure for both partners. When the ring is worn at the base of the penile shaft, its pressure creates additional engorgement of blood in the penis; the larger rings, worn over the penis and the testicles, have the same effect and produce further pressure against the man's perineal area. A common auxiliary device is a clitoral friction pad, worn in the same way as the rings but with a knurled or knobbed surface that stimulates the woman's clitoral area during intercourse. There are cuffs worn around the penis and condoms (such as the french tickler) worn over it but equipped with friction-producing surfaces that give increased vaginal stimulation.

Some primitive tribes tie bristles around the penile cuff to create extra friction. In other tribes the male inserts a device into his urethra which protrudes over the top of the glans and has the effect of a tickler. A more extreme practice involves piercing the glans itself, so that a small bone or metal *ampallang* may be inserted horizontally through the slit at the time of intercourse. In some Eastern societies it was in the past fairly common for men to have miniature bells surgically attached to the penis, just below the front of the glans. These bells provided extra friction and added a tintinnabulatory element to intercourse.

Historically the Chinese have been particularly fond of auxiliary implements inventing a number of ingenious sexual toys. One of these was the four-ball necklace, called a *konomishinju*. This necklace was inserted in the anus of one or another of the partners; during intercourse the balls would be pulled out one

at a time, with the final ball being extracted at the
moment of orgasm or, as the Chinese poetically call it,
the moment of the cloud and the rain.

The search for mechanical contrivances that may
add to the excitement or pleasure of sexual experience
is as ancient as humankind and will no doubt last as
long as the human species survives. Among recent
contributions to the list of such devices is the detach-
able, pulsating shower head, advertised for its "massag-
ing" capabilities. Sex and water have always been
associated with one another. To have sex in the
water—whether in ocean, river, pond, swimming pool,
bath, or shower—can enhance the sexual experience in
several ways. It is not merely the fact that the feel of
the water on the skin heightens sensory pleasure. The
fact of being *immersed* in water as one seeks to im-
merse oneself in the love experience is of great psychological significance. Moreover, when the body of
water is large enough, the floating sensation involved
parallels and augments the sense of lightness and
buoyancy that characterizes full entry into the love
world.

Yet, as with all sexual experience, the individual
must be prepared to deal with the increased physical
and mental stimulation provided by water. A number
of years ago I had as a patient in a mental institution a
young woman who could not accept such stimulation.
Agnes was a short woman with her hair in a bun who
walked around with a perpetual frown on her face.
When I asked her why she always frowned and why
she had been hospitalized, she replied that she had a
rat in her head. I then asked her how the rat had got
there. Agnes explained that one day while she was
taking a bath, a bright diamond-shaped light had entered her vagina. She said that it had traveled up her
spine and entered her head, where it became trans-
formed into a rat that was, she claimed, eating her
brain.

It was not until sometime later that I arrived at an interpretation of Agnes' delusion that made sense to me. From what she had told me about the "diamond-shaped light" that had entered her vagina in the bath, I came to the conclusion that she had probably been masturbating using the water faucet. Agnes came from a very strict religious background and had apparently been unable to deal with the physical pleasure that her masturbation afforded her. The thrill that she felt in her vagina was transmitted up her spinal cord. But the knowledge of the guilty pleasure of what she had done was unacceptable to her, and it continued to "eat away" at her thoughts like a rat.

Once again we can see evidence here that our sexual acts must be compatible with the way we feel about ourselves as individuals, with the way we live our lives as a whole. Agnes had been taught that sexual pleasure was forbidden outside marriage; indeed, she may have believed that women were not supposed to feel sexual pleasure at all. Thus, the physical thrill that she derived from masturbating was incompatible with what she mentally believed to be right, and the inconsistency was more than her fragile self was able to cope with.

Clearly, then, the use of mechanical devices as an adjunct to sex, whether in a masturbatory situation or in intercourse between partners, must conform to the individual's total way of living. A person who is afraid of physicality may use a fetish to distract from the direct genital contact of intercourse. But the same individual would most likely never make use of a french tickler, a device that concentrates attention on the genitals. A man who uses a penile ring to increase engorgement or endurance is likely to be quite confident of his sexual ability to begin with; if he were not, the use of the penile ring would carry for him overtones of inadequacy and might further undermine his confidence.

As we might expect, therefore, couples who make use of another kind of sexual stimulant, the mirror, are likely to have a self-approving sexual image of themselves in the first place. The use of mirrors can involve elements not only of voyeurism but also of exhibitionism and narcissism. The strong visual orientation of such partners can facilitate a heightened awareness of one another. Individuals who use mirrors are unafraid of being seen "naked," both emotionally and physically. They are at the opposite extreme from the fetishist, who tries to avert attention from genital contact; instead, through the use of mirrors, they focus explicitly on genital interaction.

Another visual stimulant is the use of pictorial representations of sexual acts. The depiction of sexual activity has a very ancient lineage, although it has been more common in some cultures than in others. As to whether such depictions are "pornographic," one must take into consideration both the intent with which the statue, drawing, photograph, or film was created and the cultural and personal attitudes of the individual who views it. In ancient India, for instance, sexuality was regarded as being an expression of the divine spirit, and explicit erotic carvings were freely exhibited side by side with more conventional religious subjects on Indian temples.

In ancient China and Japan sex manuals in the form of painted scrolls illustrating various possible positions were common. In China these scrolls were called pillow books and were widely used in the search for variety in intercourse. In Western cultures pictures of sexual activity have generally been regarded as illicit and even outright obscene. The "sexual revolution" of the last two decades has changed much of that, of course, and we are beginning to reach a degree of healthy openness about sex achieved by Eastern cultures more than 1,000 years ago!

But while the popularity of illustrated sex manuals in recent years indicates a new openness about sex, the vast amount of self-proclaimed pornography that is produced every year suggests that a great many people are particularly stimulated by pictorial representations when they are offered in a "taboo" format. As has already been noted, it had long been believed that women were not aroused by pictorial stimuli. To some extent, it is now realized, this was due to culturally induced inhibitions in women, who were taught that they should not be aroused by such material. But since many of those cultural inhibitions are still in force, the vast majority of hard-core pornographic pictures and films are produced for and used by males. In the couple relationship, therefore, it is still unusual to find the use of pornographic material. The drawings and photographs in most sex manuals, on the other hand, are presented in a manner that combines explicitness with a certain "romanticism" of style and thus have won wide acceptance for use by couples as a means for enhancing the sex experience in a mutual way. They thus serve the same purpose as the Chinese pillow books of 1,000 years ago.

Thus far in this chapter we have been dealing with the use of *objects* for sexual stimulation. The fetishist uses objects to allay anxieties concerning genital contact. Dildos, penile rings, and vibrators are used for local stimulation of body parts, particularly the genitals, and their effect is primarily a physical one. Mirrors and sexual pictures, on the other hand, have a psychophysiological effect. And we now come to a class of stimulants that are ingested into the body, usually through the mouth and that have—or are presumed to have—a physiological effect.

Sexual stimulants which are actually taken into the body include food and drink of various kinds, a wide range of drugs, and natural hormones. As we shall see, the degree to which these substances actually affect sexual arousal varies widely; some of these results, indeed, are mental—owing to a placebo effect. To begin with, there is the consumption of foods that are

deemed to have aphrodisiac qualities. There is a classic
cuisine de l'amour, whose roots go back to the beginning of recorded history.

Although various cultures have favored some foods
more than others, those that are most widely supposed
to have erotically stimulating powers include fish,
shellfish (oysters in particular), caviar, eggs, raw beef,
asparagus, mushrooms, truffles, artichokes, honey, and
chocolate. Each culture naturally tends to promote the
erotic powers of foods that are particularly associated
with its national cuisine. For instance, the renowned
French chef Jacques Manière recently stated in a
New York Times interview that if a man were to eat
a pound of truffles a day, he would become one of the
world's great lovers. He added, however, that since
truffles were so exorbitantly expensive, there were
very few great lovers to be found.

The stimulating qualities of all aphrodisiac foods
probably exist mostly in the imagination of those who
devour them, but the imagination, of course, can be
an extremely potent stimulant in itself. It is true that
during the sexual act the body is depleted of protein
and of phosphorus, and most aphrodisiac foods tend
to be high in one or the other of these components.
Seafood is especially high in phosphorus as well as
protein. For those who believe that vitamin E is an effective stimulant, raw beef is preferred to cooked,
since the vitamin E is lost in the cooking process. A
quick source of energy—for sex or anything else—is
created by the sugar in honey and chocolate. In the
case of asparagus, artichokes, mushrooms, and truffles,
apparently their musky odor has led them to be associated with sex.

Other foods appear to have erotic associations
largely for visual reasons. Thus, turtle meat is es-
teemed because of the phallic appearance of the
turtle's head, while oysters are reminiscent of testicles
and figs of the vulva. The avocado generally ranks
high as an erotic food. The Aztecs called the avocado

by their word for testicle, and according to legend, all Aztec girls were confined to the house during the height of the avocado season in order to protect their virginity. The cucumber has obvious visual connotations. It was at one time prized among the Spanish as a love food, but its associations with sex go beyond that. In France, for instance, the slang word for pimp is "cucumber," and French women sometimes use this vegetable as a genital deodorant, placing small pieces of it in the vagina. In addition, semen is sometimes described as having the flavor of cucumber.

The association of the oyster with sex, which goes back to ancient times, has turned out to be peculiarly apt, since modern research into oyster breeding has revealed that oysters lead extremely complicated sex lives. Some species are born neuter and make up their minds whether they are male or female at a later date. Others are born one sex and change to the other when they are full-grown. And some oysters never do quite make up their minds but change back and forth continuously between being male and female.

Quite aside from any presumed aphrodisiac effects, there has always been an intimate association in human societies between food and sex. This association tends to increase in proportion to the cultural sophistication of the society. Thus in primitive societies, in which food may be scarce and its procurement a matter of survival, food is more likely to be associated with religion and the offerings of foods to the gods. But in advanced civilizations, in which both food and leisure time are plentiful, the pleasures of eating and making love tend to be linked. This linkage was probably carried to its greatest extreme in the banquet orgies of the late Roman Empire, but in more refined versions it has been apparent down through the ages. During the nineteenth century the private rooms on the upper floor of the famed Lapérouse Restaurant in Paris were equipped with couches; so that the wealthy men mixing their pleasures might not be disturbed, no

waiter ever appeared without being summoned. The
association continues in our own day: A New York
food critic recently wrote an article recommending
restaurants at which adulterous or secretive lovers
might dine with the least risk of being seen and still
enjoy a romantic meal.

The idea that good food and sex go together and
that the one enhances the other thus goes beyond the
matter of any supposed chemical effect that food
might have on the body. In many cases a candlelit
meal shared by lovers can become a kind of sexual
foreplay, creating a sense of intimacy and of physical
pleasure that acts as a gateway into the love world itself. "A Jug of Wine, a Loaf of Bread—and Thou," as
Omar Khayyám has it.

The jug of wine, of course, may cause problems.
Alcohol causes a dilation of the blood vessels, not only
in the skin, which gives a feeling of warmth, but also
eventually in the sex organs. Up to a certain level of
consumption, varying from individual to individual, it
also decreases cortical inhibition of behavior. Both
these physiological effects can combine to make a person feel like having sex, but unfortunately, although it
may increase desire, alcohol tends to have the opposite
effect on actual sexual ability, often making it difficult
to achieve orgasm for both men and women and even
causing impotence in men.

Like most drugs, in fact, alcohol has differing effects on the various phases of sexual activity. Alcohol
may cause stimulation during the arousal phase but
have a debilitating effect during the plateau and orgasmic phases. As drugs in general are discussed in the
next few pages, therefore, I shall be not only reviewing their overall influence on sexual activity and
pleasure, but also pointing out the particular reactions
they cause during arousal, plateau, orgasmic, and resolution phases of coitus.

There are a number of substances that have been

used since ancient times because they were believed to increase sexual pleasure or endurance. Some of these, tested in modern times under controlled circumstances, have proved to cause various physiological changes in human beings and thus may be classified as "drugs." Others, however, have not shown such effects; like the foods considered aphrodisiacs, the sexual stimulation provided by these substances appear to be primarily a product of the users' imaginations. Two of the most popular of these supposed aphrodisiacs in the Far East, used for centuries, are ground rhinoceros horn and the Chinese plant ginseng. Rhinoceros horn is regarded as especially powerful for men, and the enormous prices that this very rare and rather bizarre commodity fetches recently led to the arrest of a Japanese supplier who was trafficking in a counterfeit substance. Ginseng is plentiful and relatively cheap. Its users claim that ginseng contributes to overall sexual health and performance, a contention difficult to prove or disprove. Neither ginseng nor rhinoceros horn, however, has been shown to have any readily detectable physiological effects.

In central Africa native tribes use yohimbine, derived from the bark of the yohimbé tree, to increase sexual powers. This drug increases the excitability of the lower centers of the spinal cord, as well as causes hyperemia—extra blood in the genital organs. Another drug with definite—and dangerous—physiological effects is cantharis, the famous so-called Spanish fly. Cantharides are derived from a beautiful sheen-covered beetle found in southern Europe, the cantharis. The beetles are anesthetized, dried, and then heated until they disintegrate into a fine powder. When cantharides are taken internally, there is a resulting acute irritation of the gastrointestinal system. In addition, the genitourinary tract becomes inflamed, and the accompanying dilation of the blood vessels stimulates the genitals. The results of this "urethral excitement" can be sexual in nature. Cantharides can

cause priapism—a continued erection without sexual
desire—in the male or premature menstruation in the
female. Large doses have been known to cause internal
bleeding and subsequent death. They are thus extremely dangerous.

Drugs like yohimbine and cantharis obviously will
affect all phases of the sexual cycle. But because of the
fact that the stimulation is caused by irritation and
emphasizes the purely genital aspects of sex, these
drugs are likely to distort, rather than enhance, the
overall experience. What is more, because their effect
will continue after orgasm, the resolution phase is
negated and with it the sense of satisfaction and completion of the normal sex experience.

Some drugs or other substances are used externally
rather than internally and have a milder and more
controllable effect on sexual excitement. Oil of wintergreen, for instance, is a local irritant that increases
the hyperemia of the genitals. It may be applied
directly to the genitals or held in the mouth of the
partner during fellatio or cunnilingus. In order to prevent destructive irritation, it is used in highly diluted
concentrations. Nupercaine, a derivative of cocaine, is
used for an entirely opposite reason. It produces a local anesthesia and is sometimes applied to the frenulum or glans of the penis to prevent premature
ejaculation in those suffering from this dysfunction.
Oil of wintergreen is thus appropriate for use in the
arousal or plateau phase to increase stimulation, while
Nupercaine, by inhibiting ejaculation, makes it possible for some men to get beyond the arousal phase
and to maintain an erection long enough to bring both
themselves and their partners through the full cycle of
sexual response.

Although cocaine derivatives act as an anesthetic
when applied externally, cocaine itself sometimes augments the sexual drive when taken internally. In a
study by George R. Gay and Charles W. Sheppard, it
is reported that ten out of twenty males who had in-

jected cocaine intravenously achieved erection simultaneously with injection. Two of these men, it should be added, reported that injection led to painful episodes of priapism, lasting more than twenty-four hours.

In the same study it was found that amphetamines, used intravenously, also augmented the sexual drive. For ten of eighteen males, erection occurred simultaneously with injection, and for three out of eighteen females, orgasm took place upon injection. Another report, however, showed that amphetamine addiction produced no effect on sexuality in five cases, decreased desire in three cases, and an increase in both desire and erotic sensation in five cases.

Unfortunately there are no in-depth studies in which the overall sexual attitudes and practices of those studied are correlated with their drug use. But one might speculate that people who undertake the acquisition of illegal drugs for the purposes of injection are likely to suffer from some kind of sexual difficulty, since such hard-drug users usually suffer from a variety of personality disturbances. Thus it seems likely that a considerable number of those who report sexual arousal following injection are using the drugs in part to open the way into the love world, a way that is ordinarily blocked for them. This theory would appear to be borne out by the fact that those who use both amphetamines and cocaine often save the more expensive cocaine specifically for sexual stimulation.

The data concerning heroin users are more extensive in respect to sexual responses. One study shows that heroin addicts feel little sexual desire and engage in less than average overt sexual activity. During sex they show a marked decrease in sensitivity, which is demonstrated particularly in the extended time required to ejaculate and the poor quality of the orgasm for both men and women. The fact that the use of heroin reduces psychological discomfort relating to the experience of sexual inadequacy may serve, indeed, to reinforce the use of the drug. Since heroin may weaken or interfere with sexual arousal in the addict, it can in effect function to *prevent* the person from engaging in sexual behavior with its associated discomfort. If sexual behavior or desire is accompanied by anxiety, the heroin could also act as an anesthetic, thus *permitting* the addict to have encounters without experiencing such strong feelings of anxiety. In general, the use of heroin results in a relative loss of sexuality and a diminished frequency of intercourse, masturbation, and nocturnal emissions. It is interesting to note that because of its sedative effect, heroin allows prostitutes with severe psychological problems to perform their activity with minimum pressure and strain.

Two drugs with a much more widespread use in our society are amyl nitrite and marijuana. Amyl nitrite is a drug used medicinally to combat angina—cardiac pain—by temporarily increasing the blood supply to the heart musculature. But it is also widely used, in the form of "poppers" for its rush of sexual excitement. Although amyl nitrite should be used only under medical control, it has become so popular that there are numerous substitutes on the market that have not yet come under the control of the Food and Drug Administration and are freely advertised in magazines. The substitutes, however, do not have as powerful a "kick" as amyl nitrite itself. Amyl nitrite is inhaled, usually by breaking a small ampul or by saturating a piece of cotton that is first placed in an ordinary inhaler. It is most often used at arousal or at the point of orgasm. By increasing the blood supply in general to various parts of the body, it creates a heightened level of excitement.

With marijuana the case is more complicated. There is an increasing number of studies of the effects of marijuana, and the results are often conflicting. Thus one study says that it reduces sexual desire—and another reports that in forty out of fifty cases it increases sexual pleasure. But perhaps this is not truly a contradiction, if we look at the matter in terms of the sexual phases. It is quite possible that even though *desire*—the arousal stage—is reduced, the plateau, orgasmic, and resolution phases might be enhanced once sexual activity was actually initiated. It is generally agreed that marijuana acts on the higher centers of the brain to reduce inhibitions and usual restraints on behavior. Thus, although it may not stimulate physical arousal, it may make the sexual experience more relaxed and spontaneous for those who do have sex under its influence.

Marijuana seems to allow detours in the customary channels of experience and permit the transcendence of some social inhibitions. User attitudes toward marijuana may thus determine what happens to their bodies when they smoke it. Rather than have a specific effect on the human physiology, the marijuana experience appears to reflect the established self. Those who expect increased sexual pleasure are likely to experience it, and such people characterize sexual experience under the drug's influence as especially intense, long, sensuous, and pleasurable. It should be noted, however, that marijuana users are in general more sexually permissive than nonusers to begin with. The picture is much the same for those who take hallucinogens—LSD, STP, or MDA. By removing inhibitions and affecting certain sensations or perceptual effects, these drugs can give those who initiate sex a heightened experience. There is some evidence that MDA actually stimulates arousal as well.

There is a further confusion concerning marijuana. A study by Robert C. Kolodny provides evidence that in males who are chronic and intensive users of marijuana there is a depression in the level of plasma testosterone. Testosterone is the male sex hormone and is primarily produced in the testicles of the male. It is also present to a lesser extent in the female, where it is produced in the liver, the adrenal glands, and a number of other organs. In chronic male users of marijuana, testosterone was found to be reduced but rebounded to normal levels once the marijuana use was curtailed. Thus, while users may claim heightened sexual pleasure or drive, the data in this study suggest the possibility of adverse effects on male sexual functioning. It should be pointed out that testosterone in itself is sometimes prescribed for use by males whose natural production of the hormone is below normal levels. Once the normal level is reached, however, additional doses of the hormone will not increase sexual drive further; in women the administration of testosterone creates virilization—the additional growth of body hair, for instance.

Kolodny suggests that the effects of marijuana on testosterone levels need further study. Since testosterone in the female plays a part in the sexual differentiation of the fetus, marijuana use by pregnant women could affect the fetus at critical stages of its sexual development. Additionally, there is the possibility that use by prepubertal males could delay the advent of puberty.

Finally, in regard to drugs, it is important to note that certain ordinary prescription drugs can affect sexual drive and performance. Tranquilizers, antihypertensive drugs, and stimulants of various sorts, prescribed by physicians to treat common medical problems unrelated to sex, do sometimes have side effects which cause a change in the libido. No one is likely to complain if sexual interest is increased, but the opposite reaction can cause considerable distress.

Interestingly, male patients are more likely to complain of these side effects than are women. One woman who began taking a drug to combat her high blood pressure told her physician that since she had started taking the drug she had noticed a sharp drop-off in her sexual arousal and interest. The physician told her that although a number of men had come to him about problems of this kind, she was the first woman who had ever spoken up. There are probably two reasons for this fact. First, some antihypertensive drugs can cause actual—and very noticeable—impotence in the male, while the slackening of the female drive is less blatantly obvious. Secondly, it may be that the old cultural stereotypes are at work here, with many women reluctant to report problems relating to sexual interest and drive. Fortunately there are a variety of antihypertensive drugs, which affect different individuals in different ways, and it is almost always possible to remedy such side effects with the use of a different drug or combination of drugs. But anyone who notices a considerable change in his or her degree of sexual arousal when taking a prescription drug would be well advised to bring the matter up with his or her physician.

All the variations on a theme that have been discussed in this chapter—fetishes, mechanical devices, water, mirrors, aphrodisiacs, drugs, and hormones— share a common meaning in respect to the sex experience. Although on the surface most of them appear to be directed at enhancing or stimulating the physical aspects of sex, their use is more profound than that. Just as the true fetishist finds it impossible to enjoy sex or enter the love world at all except through use of the fetish, individuals making use of these various devices and techniques are seeking ways to experience the love transcendence. It does not matter whether they are used to distance the individual from the sexual experience, and so allay anxiety, or to bring the experience closer, so as to comprehend it more completely; whatever the need, whatever the motive, the result that is being sought is a transcendence of the ordinary world and the fullest possible envelopment in the love world.

CHAPTER 11

Fantastics

Sexual fantasy is a universal outgrowth of being human. In fact, the ability to project ourselves into situations that have not happened, and may never happen, is one of the things that distinguishes us from all other animals. Yet the kind of fantasies that we have, and the purposes to which we put them, may differ extraordinarily from person to person. One person's pleasurable fantasy may be another's dreaded nightmare. Like all our other modes of being in the world, our fantasies define our uniqueness as individuals.

Fantasy originates in the imagination; in fact, the word for "imagination" in German is *Phantasie*. In psychoanalytic and psychological terms, fantasies are mental productions that take place during the day. Dr. Jerome L. Singer has divided these "daydreams" into four major categories. Some individuals have anxious or distracted daydreams and take little pleasure in the practice. A second group has guilty daydreams, which may show a combination of great striving for achievement and a marked fear of failure. Whether they are men or women, people in this group appear to be strongly oriented toward masculine concerns in our society. A third group has "happy" daydreams, positive, vivid, and oriented toward the future. A fourth, less common group has daydreams of an objective and thoughtfully controlled nature.

The fantasies of any given individual, I have found, fall into specific patterns that exactly reflect the emotional content of that person's life. There are some fantasies that are so common as to be nearly universal—known to analysts by such names as the oedipal fantasy, the beating fantasy, the family romance fantasy, etc. Yet even these common fantasies, despite the similarity of their general format, will be filled in by each individual with details that make the daydream unique to that person. The degree to which human beings are able to make a particular fantasy their own is illustrated by a literary experiment of a number of years ago. A publisher gave a dozen well-known writers a brief plot outline and asked each of them to write a short story using the characters and situations provided. Yet none of the twelve stories was at all alike, so varied were the points of view from which the different writers approached the given situation. Indeed, each writer found a different "meaning" in the events described.

Fantasies with sexual content may occur at a very young age. But it is not until early adolescence that young people begin to have fantasies that they would recognize as sexual. Usually, such sexual fantasies occur in boys about two years later than they do in girls. Girls tend to have idealized fantasies with a "Prince Charming" theme, imagining a lover who will take care of them and change their lives. It may be that with the ongoing changes in sexual and social mores, the fantasies of young girls are also changing somewhat. In general, however, girls fantasize about being loved, while boys fantasize about engaging in sex and the seduction of females. Perhaps because their fantasies are less explicit than those of boys, girls share them with their peers more than boys do.

A frequent way in which both sexes express their sexual fantasies is through their use with masturbation. From puberty onward, human beings use fantasy as a way of entering the love world. Long before the teenager has had any actual experience of intercourse, he or she imagines a partner, seeking through fantasy the desired unity and sense of transcendence. Some young people, of course, become trapped in their fantasies. Their imaginary sexual encounters are "safer" and less challenging than intercourse with an actual partner, and the real experience may be postponed well into the twenties or beyond when anxieties concerning intimacy, physicality, or commitment inhibit the person from establishing adult sexual relationships.

Fantasies, however, should not be seen as being in *opposition* to reality. They may sometimes be substituted for reality, but more often they are used in ways that enable the individual to open up additional aspects of the world. Fantasies exist at all levels and through all phases of the love experience. They play a particularly active part in the initial crystallization of love. As individuals fall in love, they use fantasy to bring the desired partner closer to the center of their lives. Because fantasies transcend chronological time, they open up to the fantasist the possibility of living in an expanded world that includes the partner.

Studies by Dr. Singer and Dr. Barbara Hariton have confirmed that many ordinary women, suburban housewives, have fantasies while engaged in intercourse with their husbands. Their fantasies commonly involve images of romantic lovers, being forced to surrender, reliving previous sexual experiences, the idea of delighting many men, or imagining that they are observing themselves or others having sex. Those who have positive and vivid daydreams are particularly likely to have fantasies during coitus. Generally they do not report dissatisfaction with their husbands; rather, their erotic fantasies are "a natural continuation of their predisposition to elaborate and enrich all kinds of experience through fantasy." The anxious daydreamers were found more likely to express dissatisfaction with their husbands and with the sexual act in general. Some women imagined infidelity during intercourse itself. But interestingly, some of these women regarded themselves as happily married; others did not. In both cases the fantasies were used to stimulate arousal or bring on orgasm.

There is very little evidence concerning fantasies during intercourse on the part of men. From my own experience with patients, it is clear that these do sometimes occur but probably less often than in women. There are indications that men who are particularly active, controlling the sexual pattern, are less likely to have such fantasies, perhaps because their attention is so strongly focused on the physicality of the encounter.

In connection with male fantasies, there is some significant data about paraplegic men. Because of the disruption in the spinal cord, impulses from higher nervous centers can no longer travel down to the genitals. But reflex centers at the genital level continue to operate automatically—that is, direct genital stimulation will produce a reflex erection. However, the sensation of ejaculation at orgasm cannot be felt, and therefore the pleasure of orgasm is not experienced. Here we have an example of the body's way of being in the world existing at variance with the mental way of being in the world. That is, the body can be aroused and will react, but the mental experience of that arousal is neutral or to a certain extent detached. Yet many paraplegics compensate for this difficulty in entering the love world in their sleeping dreams, in which they experience particularly vivid and voluptuous orgasms—although in this case the body does not react and there is no actual ejaculation.

Fantasy can provide a gateway into the love world. A paraplegic dreams his orgasms. A suburban housewife may imagine another lover in order to achieve orgasm. But for fantasy to have a positive effect on the individual's experience of the love world, it must be combined with an equal and parallel emphasis upon the bodily and behavioral aspects of sexuality. When the individual concentrates on fantasy alone and the

love world experience becomes overloaded by fantasies, there is a danger of the individual's being out of
balance. These imbalances generally occur when there
is an excess of inhibition or prohibition in the behavioral and physiological areas of response, resulting
from training, situation, neurosis or physical limitations.

A female patient of mine provides a good example
of what can happen when the way into the love
world comes to be dominated by fantasy. This
woman's daily life was consumed by fantasy. A large
part of her daytime existence was given over to fantasies concerning past sexual activity—so much so that
it affected the efficiency of her work. While having
intercourse with her husband, she would continue to
have fantasies about other men. She behaved coquettishly in circumstances involving men, whether at work
or in social situations, and would create flirtatious
relationship in a fledgling attempt to act out her
fantasies.

During therapeutic treatment it was found that the
origin of her fantasies lay in seductions by adult males
during her childhood, which had resulted in an enormous overloading of her then-limited controls. She
had been a very pretty child, and the postman, for example, used to fondle her when he delivered the mail.
Her dentist and an older male relative would do the
same. Once these sources of her fantasy life had been
uncovered in therapy, it led to the elimination or inhibition of her fantasies, although she was in no way
prohibited from using fantasy. The efficiency of her
work improved as she fantasized less, but for a while
she experienced increased difficulties in her sexual
reactivity during actual intercourse. She had dispensed
with the neurotic use of fantasy in sex but had not
worked her problems through completely enough to
be able as yet to function freely sexually without
them. A neurotic fantasy life had been her way into
the love world, and now she had to find a new way

based on a freer sexual self. For some time she frequently looked back with nostalgia upon her previous fantasy use, which had enabled her to achieve orgasm.

One of the most common uses of fantasy in the sexual area is to overcome inhibitions—particularly the inability to reach orgasm, as shown by the above example. The use of fantasy to facilitate orgasm during masturbation or intercourse can take many forms, however. Very often the source of the fantasy may be voyeuristic activity, the individual masturbating while looking at pornographic pictures or even the photograph of a movie star. In psychoanalytic work the analysis of such fantasies is important because it gives a clear understanding of the dimensions and content of the individual's sexual and emotional life.

When a loved person does not in actuality exist or is not physically present, the physical absence may be overcome during masturbation by the use of mental imagining. One young man with practically no experience of the opposite sex would masturbate only after seeing an idealized woman on the street. He would use the image of this woman in his masturbatory fantasy. However, no matter how hard he tried, he would be unable to retain her image in his mind beyond the plateau phase; her image would have to be wiped out before he could achieve orgasm. In his way of living there was such a strong prohibition or inhibition relating to sexual activity that he could enter the love world only in a physical way, unable to experience sexual intimacy—not even in a mental way.

The degree to which fantasies delineate the actual dimensions and extent of the individual's love and sex universe are further demonstrated by a young man whose problem took a form exactly opposite to the case discussed above. This young man was an only son who had a very close relationship with his mother. When masturbating, he could achieve orgasm only if at the point of orgasmic inevitability he had a mental image of an older woman who was a friend of his mother's. In therapy, as the young man began to understand the oedipal implications of this fantasy image, he tried to eliminate the image. Yet inescapably, at the moment that he approached orgasm, the image of the older woman would slip unbidden into his mind, and ejaculation would immediately occur. In spite of his continual vigilance and struggle against it, the image always appeared.

Sometimes a person is so severely inhibited that the sexual element will be absent altogether from the fantasy. One male patient had been born with a rare hereditary bone disease, and numerous plastic surgery operations had been necessary to overcome the physical deficiencies involved. He had an extremely poor image of himself and had to find a way to counteract it when he masturbated. He was not homosexual, but his fantasy involved seeing a handsome young man dressed in a military school uniform. He did not imagine himself having sexual relations with this young man; rather, he used this positive image to blot out the negative image he had of himself. Only through such substitution could he achieve final release.

All these cases involve the fulfillment of special conditions for the love unity; one man imagines an unobtainable but desirable woman, another a substitute for his mother, another a substitute for himself. But more important, the images are used as a way of making it possible for the particular person to experience love. And in each case the particular nature of the fantasy exactly corresponds to the basic life situation of the individual. As with all other aspects of sexuality—initiation, positions, patterns or response, vocalization, the need for light or darkness—the fantasies of a given person reflect that man or woman's way of being in the world.

A great many fantasies have a sadistic or masochistic character. Masochistic fantasies have in the past been particularly common among women, in large part because of cultural conditioning. The Victorian dictum that women were not supposed to enjoy sex but that they were nevertheless "duty-bound" to "permit" their husbands to engage in sexual intercourse according to the husband's desires has influenced sexual attitudes during most of the twentieth century, and such a dictum obviously creates a situation in which female masochistic fantasies would be virtually inevitable.

A typical masochistic fantasy was related by the same young female patient who was so excited by the illustration of cunnilingus. In her masochistic fantasy, wine was spilled over her and licked off by a shabby, uncouth older male. She further imagined that she was tied down and could not protest. This fantasy had originated in her previously described relationship with a somewhat seductive stepfather. The shabby and uncouth appearance of the male clearly shows her value judgment that the fantasy seduction was dirty. Yet it retained such a hold on her imagination that she saw herself as powerless, helplessly bound and unable to defend herself against it.

Masochistic fantasies also occur to males, however. In one case a young man fantasized that he was tied to a conveyor belt, like that on an assembly line, which transported him over a line of beautiful women. The apparatus would lower him on a woman, and coitus would occur, with the woman taking the active part. The machine would then carry him on to the next voluptuary.

In both masochistic and sadistic fantasies, individuals may be disturbed by the nature of their own fantasies, yet still be aroused by them. A study carried out by Günter Schmidt at the University of Hamburg clearly shows that arousal and emotional acceptance of the arousing stimuli do not necessarily coincide.

During one phase of this wide-ranging study the participants were shown four different films. One film depicted a sadomasochistic ritual, the second included a scene of two women flagellating one another, the

third showed a group rape, and the fourth involved
nonaggressive sex. The reactions of the participants
were monitored by a variety of devices that were capable of recording objective, physical signs of sexual
arousal. Not only can such physiological responses as
blood pressure, heart rate, and respiration be gauged,
but specific genital response can also be measured. In
men, a penile pressure cuff is used. In women, another
device is used to record the swelling of the vagina and
to detect vaginal lubrication.

The male and female reactions to the four films
were found to be quite similar. For both men and
women, the strongest arousal was to the nonaggressive
film, which was shown as a control against which to
measure the responses to the aggressive films. Both
males and females responded to the sadomasochistic
film with low arousal, strong emotional avoidance, an
anxious mood, and with moderate signs of ag-
gressiveness. But it is the reaction to the rape film that
is most interesting. Here both men and women responded with relatively high arousal *but also* strong
emotional avoidance, anxiety, and much ag-
gressiveness. The type of conflict experienced in response to this film differed somewhat between men
and women. In the women the film produced sexual
arousal and—because of identification with the vic-
tim—fears of being overpowered. However, the conflict in the men was characterized by guilt feelings
and dismay at being stimulated by aggressive sexual
activity that was incompatible with their conscious
standards of sexuality.

The evidence of the Schmidt study corresponds to
the evidence derived from therapy with patients. The
Schmidt volunteers found themselves aroused by rape
scenes of which they disapproved, just as the young
man who envisioned the older woman who was his
mother's friend was aroused by the image even
though he tried to prevent it from entering his
thoughts. Yet—and it is important to be clear about

this—no person can or will be aroused by sexual acts or fantasies that lie beyond the bounds of that individual's potential sexual landscape. That is one reason why rape is so disturbing. Even as the thought of rape is abhorrent, it is nevertheless sexually stimulating to many people—men and women—who would prefer not to recognize that they can be aroused by an aggressive sexual act. Rape is a way of forcibly entering the love world for men and of being forced to enter the love world for women. Entrance into the love world brings transcendence, and the idea of force may seem incompatible with that sense of elevation. Yet the need for transcendence runs so deep in human beings that the connection between transcendence and force, at least in fantasy, retains a secret power to move human beings sexually.

In most cases, of course, forcible, incestuous, sadistic, or masochistic sexual acts remain in the realm of fantasy. The acting out of fantasy, of transforming the thought into behavior, raises other problems, of course. In many cases the acting out of a fantasy involves only masturbatory behavior. For instance, one middle-aged masochistic man would arrange pieces of wood in the form of a cross and then tie himself to this crucifix. He would have prepared, in addition, a rope, one end of which was tied around his neck and the other attached to his penis. With a periodic rhythm he would flex and unflex his head, tightening and untightening the rope, thus masturbating while at the same time he imagined himself to be Jesus on the Cross.

Another patient of mine carried his fantasy over into the outside world, however. This man was married, the father of small children. But overwhelmed by a dominating father-in-law for whom he worked, he had lost all sexual drive in regard to his wife. By acting out a fantasy, he found a substitute way to have sexual experience and to enter the love world. Wearing tight-fitting pants, he would ride the subways, exhibiting his erection, clearly outlined within the taut cloth, to a woman sitting opposite him. He would watch the uncomfortable woman to see her trapped reaction to this aggressive act. He would carry this experience with him when he got off the subway, find the nearest free toilet booth, and masturbate with her image in mind.

There were reasons why this behavior took place on the subway. As a child he had found that his brother was given more attention and love by his mother. The burning rage of the sibling rivalry was so strong that he had once set fire to his brother's baby carriage. He was not psychotic and had enough control to do this when the baby was not in the carriage, acting out his rage without injuring the child. But he did have a loving grandmother, whom he adored, and as a teenager and young man he would ride the subway every weekend to see her. Thus, for him, the subway was experienced as a conduit to love.

Another patient of mine became involved in a situation in which the limits of the sexual imagination became extraordinarily extended. My patient was a bisexual man, whom I will call Mark. He had a woman friend, Ann, and they sometimes had sex together. He began to think, timorously, of a possible love relationship between them in addition to a transient sexual one. However, this proved to be impossible because Ann was also involved with a man who had a gender-identity problem. After a short period this man underwent a sex-change operation and became a woman, continuing the relationship with Ann but now in a homosexual context. But living as a woman physically, the transsexual now found the need to have a relationship with a man, and she left Ann. Unfortunately this liaison proved to be full of conflict, and she ultimately committed suicide.

In the interim Ann had turned once again to my patient, Mark, and there was a moderate intensification of both the sexual and the love relationship between them. But Ann did not find their affair fully satisfying and married another bisexual man. On the wedding night Mark had sex thirteen times—five or six times with the bride, three or four times with the groom, twice with the best man, with the maid of honor, and with assorted guests. This feat of stamina was made possible by the energizing sexual arousal derived from the acting out of an orgiastic oedipal sexual fantasy.

Many of the case histories in this chapter have involved the use of sexual fantasy for masturbatory purposes. That is their most common usage. But we have also seen that fantasy is used during actual coitus as well. An article on women's fantasies by Marc Hollender points out that through fantasy the woman may draw away from the partner. When the woman concentrates on her fantasy, the man's physical presence and activity can become relatively insignificant; *her* thinking and *her* physical reaction then become the focal point of the experience. In this way, according to Hollender, sexual intercourse can become converted into a form of masturbation.

These observations may be extended in terms of what happens in the context of the love world. The unity of the love world is clearly disrupted when fantasy is used excessively during intercourse; the partners are not achieving transcendence *through* one another but *in spite of* one another. But it must be remembered that for many people the use of fantasy is necessary in order to enter the love world at all. Thus sexual partners who use fantasy to a large extent during intercourse may be using the only means available to them through which to achieve transcendence. The love unity may not be fully achieved because of the distancing of the partner that is taking place. Yet from the perspective of the fantasizing individual, entrance into the love world is being achieved in at least some measure, whereas it might not occur at all without the use of fantasy.

CHAPTER 12

Sexual Insight and Destiny: Finding New Fulfillment

The theme of this book has been that the sex positions chosen by individuals—positions that are preferred, spontaneously assumed, and used with pleasure and effectiveness—are expressions of the individual's essential way of living. How the person prefers to behave in the sexual relationship is another facet of the fundamental, characteristic way in which the person behaves in other areas of daily life that may be of a more mundane nature. Viewing the couple relationship, we can see that the positions chosen, the patterns of rhythm and release, and the functional interaction throughout coitus represent that particular couple's unified way of living together as partners.

This means, of course, that if the couple experiences difficulty in the sex-love duality, parallel difficulties are likely to exist in other aspects of their relationship. If intimacy and spontaneity are lacking in the sexual encounter, their lack usually will be felt throughout the relationship as a whole. Yet exactly because the couple's ways of behaving together are manifested so concretely in their sexual choices, an analysis of their sex positions and patterns can help them recognize more clearly the elements in their overall relationship that are strong and those that may need strengthening. And such recognition can be half the battle in overcoming problems in a love-sex partnership.

In psychotherapy the first step toward making changes in a person's way of living involves the perception of one's self, where one comes from, and how one relates to others—the basic principles that form the individual life-style. Today most people have some grasp of the fundamentals of human psychology, and many individuals are quick to make an amateur "analysis" of the problems of a friend. But we are usually not objective about ourselves or about those to whom we are emotionally close. In order to arrive at an understanding of ourselves, we must often eliminate our own blind spots and resistances. But through an analysis of our sexual patterns and choices we gain the possibility of grasping in a direct and incontrovertible manner the concrete evidence that we live in particular ways.

The statements concerning the couple relationship that are made by sex positions and patterns are so simple, direct, immediate, and easily grasped that it is possible to understand the essential nature of the couple's interaction without resorting to complicated tests, interviews, and procedures. Here is evidence that we can see and feel; it is tangible. We can recognize ourselves more fully for the individuals we are and can see our feelings about our partners clearly spelled out in the sex-love interaction. If we should see, for instance, that a certain lack of intimacy exists in our choice of positions, we will have immediately gained in our understanding of ourselves and the nature of the relationship. Our sexual behavior can thus provide us with clues that can be used as a basis for opening ourselves to the possibilities of new realms of experience and new ways of relating. Every time a new comprehension of ourselves or our relationships emerges we have begun to change. New knowledge is in itself change. Having understood the significance of our actions, we can use this knowledge to custom-tailor our potentials for change to our own individual natures and needs.

We have seen that individuals have preferred sexual positions. But we have also seen that in the transports of passion, individuals and couples can transcend what is merely comfortable or habitual and extend the lim-

its of their ordinary behavioral horizons. The person
who fears intimacy can sometimes during the ecstasy
of sex find release from the anxieties that usually prevent a full face-to-face open encounter with others.
Let us assume that a couple usually has intercourse in
the Crossbow position, with the man on top of the
woman but at right angles to her, as was the case with
one of my patients. The man's position shows a reluc-
tance to align himself fully and directly with the
woman. But if occasionally, released and transported
by the love experience, he finds himself able to bring
himself face to face with his partner in the full missionary position—even momentarily—then we have evidence that such intimacy is possible for him, that it
can be achieved. Understanding the significance of
this change in position may make it possible for the
man also to attempt the achievement of closer alignment in other areas of the relationship.

In my study of sleep positions I noted that the ability to assume a new sleep position was contingent
upon assuming a new position in life. In order to enter
the sleep world, the individual must surrender controlled consciousness, so that it is usually impossible to
"direct" oneself while in the sleep world. One may,
before falling asleep, attempt a new position, yet as
sleep comes, one will finally revert to the old position
that brings with it the greatest security and thus
makes sleep possible. But with sex positions there is a
new element involved. We are aware of what we are
doing when we have sex and are able deliberately to
direct or manipulate the action. Thus, we have, as a
built-in factor, the ability to vary, to experiment, to
change—to try new positions and attitudes, new
rhythms, new accents, and new colorations.

Furthermore, even the most rigid individual—the
person whose anxieties make it difficult to tolerate sex
except in a controlled and routine way—will at times
vary some elements of the sexual encounter. The
creativity of human beings is ever-present and may
often triumph over even the most deep-seated inhibi-

tions. For most of us, in fact, the urge to experiment, to try something new, is constantly at work. In sexual relations this *novelty factor* also carries with it the possibility of increasing pleasure. Thus, in sex there are always two factors operating simultaneously. We have our preferred mode, growing out of our need to feel secure, while at the same time there is a search for variety. And when we do try something new or different—and find it stimulating and pleasurable—there is a feedback mechanism that gives us the desire to try other variations.

If an attempt is made consciously to push behavior to the edge of the possible or beyond it into previously unexplored areas, then the individual can establish new paths, new ways of moving out into the world. When a person is afraid to try a new position or technique, it is usually for one of two reasons. The individual may personally feel that the desired act is shameful or repugnant. Or the individual may be inhibited in this preference because of anxiety that expressing such desire would bring about the condemnation of the partner. Even in the wake of the sexual revolution, many partners continue to be reticent about trying certain sexual activities.

Because reticence to act in a physical way is almost invariably accompanied by an equally strong inhibition about discussing sexual possibilities openly, this dual lack of communication, both physical and verbal, may be obscuring opportunities for increased pleasure for both partners. For most people, though, it is likely to be easier to attempt physically the new or different at the height of arousal than to suggest it verbally. To say, "I'd like to try something different," requires a great deal of trust between partners; simply *doing* it may be the easier path. But it should also be understood that if the partner actively resists the new maneuver, the resistance grows out of that person's particular ways of being in the world.

If a person has inhibitions in some sexual area, desired change can still be effected through the use of unblocking techniques to achieve greater sexual and emotional freedom. A person who prefers the rear-entry position because it is favorable to detachment and control can make a conscious decision to try another position, such as the missionary, in a voluntary attempt to give up some degree of control in the love relationship and to strive for greater intimacy. There may be some resistance and anxiety in trying a new position—in extreme cases even a loss of erection in the male or lubrication in the female. But that anxiety can gradually be decreased by trying the new position for only a few moments in the course of coitus and then returning to the preferred position. The man who prefers rear entry might begin copulation in that position and then, when fully aroused, change to the missionary position briefly during the plateau phase. In order to achieve orgasm, it may be necessary to return to the rear-entry position. But if the missionary position is assumed for a brief time on each occasion that the couple makes love, the anxiety may gradually be diminished, so that the new position can be assumed for longer periods. Ultimately it might be possible to achieve orgasm consistently in the new position.

I have previously noted that where sexual dissension exists between partners, it often revolves around the question of who will be on top. The same general unblocking technique can be used to resolve this situation, with the woman astride for part of the time and the man on top at other intervals. Eventually both partners should find themselves less resistant to the position desired by the other. Furthermore, many of the positions set forth in this book have certain elements of "compromise" built into them. The analyses I have presented should make it possible for the couple to select positions that move in a new direction but do not involve a drastic change or require full commitment to a way of behaving that causes anxiety.

For example, if both the man and the woman prefer to be on top, they might try the Sling position. Here, although the woman is astride, the man is using his arms to support her and there is considerable equality involved in the verticality of both bodies. Thus, the man has considerably greater control than if he were supine, while the woman is given the opportunity to retain many of the significant elements of the basic woman-astride position.

If the man prefers rear entry while the woman prefers the missionary position, an occasional compromise might be reached by using the South Pacific position. Here the woman is supine, as she would be in the missionary position. But although he is now facing the woman, the man retains a great deal of the control he would have in the rear-entry position, and since he is vertically at right angles to the woman, there is a large degree of the detachment that he still needs.

New love potentials can thus be achieved in two different ways. A completely new position can be assumed for brief periods. Or a compromise position may be attempted on occasion. Similar techniques can be applied to other areas of the sexual encounter. I have pointed out that some men have sexual conflicts that make it difficult for them to take pleasure in a woman's genitals except in a tactile way and thus may be strongly resistant to the practice of cunnilingus. Some women find the act of fellatio equally negative. If one partner desires such oral means of pleasure, the reluctant partner can work to overcome his or her own anxiety by gradual steps.

To begin with, a simple genital kiss may be used occasionally, with the lips closed and no use of the tongue. The kiss need last only a second at first, but it is likely that the partner's pleasure in this action, combined with the realization on the part of the active partner that there is nothing to fear from it, will eventually make it possible for actual cunnilingus or fellatio to take place without disturbance. This technique can also work in the opposite situation, as when one partner wishes to perform oral sex but the other has anxieties concerning this form of arousal. In this case the active partner must take care not to go too far too quickly.

The use of these unblocking techniques brings up an important point. If both partners are sexually inhibited in the same areas, it is far more difficult to effect change, but since neither partner desires it, there is at least no conflict. In most cases, however, when one partner is blocked, the other may be less so, or their restraints may exist in different areas. In these situations the partner who is more open in the particular sexual area can serve as a potent guide or catalyst in the attempt to explore new behavior potentials. What is required in such cases is patience, gentleness, and an understanding that the partner's difficulty in responding is not usually a deliberate act but rather embodies the sexual aspect of his or her overall way of behaving in the world. Change must not be demanded but gradually created.

In suggesting these methods for broadening one's sexual horizons, I do so in the framework of the love world concept. Some sex manuals include sections suggesting the use of bondage or group sex to add spice to the sexual diet. I suspect that most couples who would find such practices enjoyable are already engaged in them. For some other couples, these sexual alternatives could obviously be destructive. As I have made clear previously, sexual devices may be required by certain people in order for them to enter the love world at all. But the use of such devices limits the extent to which the sex-love transcendence can be achieved. This is also true, of course, for group sex. It is difficult enough for two people to achieve unity, and when you add a third or a fourth, the situation takes on the aspects of an emotional jigsaw puzzle. Thus, in the advocacy of experimentation and change, it is with the object of helping couples to achieve a richer love experience, not a more attenuated one. It is to be hoped, therefore, that couples will seek to change in directions that enhance the intimacy, spontaneity, physicality, pleasure, and commitment in the relationship.

On the other hand, this is not to say that couples should be afraid to try certain of the described positions because they reflect, for instance, seemingly extreme domination by one partner or the other. The complexity of human relationships is such that there is room for many different patterns of relationship through which love can be realized. If a couple wishes to assume the Wheelbarrow or Lotus positions as an experiment, to do so is merely to recognize that their relationship is able to encompass the elements shown by the chosen position. If they try the Wheelbarrow on one occasion and the Lotus on another, the relationship is clearly one in which neither partner fears domination by the other—or requires it. Rather, there is a sense of mutual trust that makes it possible for either partner to assume dominance at certain times without the other succumbing to anxiety.

To comprehend the significance of our sexual behavior creates the basis for a condition in which it is possible to alter the direction of our life journey as a whole. Human beings are anything but puppets or robots manipulated by blind energies and drives. Rather, we are always trying to move toward the state of transcendence that is implicit in the love-sex relationship, and the more completely we grasp the essence of its meaning, the greater are our chances of achieving it. With this perspective we can reach toward that broadening of experience, that melting of detachment, that thrill of pleasure, and that closeness of body, heart, and mind that constitute the love world. Each time we make love we are reaching out, striving with all our being to achieve the totality of transcendence. Yet our progression toward the experience of this transcendence is always open to enrichment. We make love; we create it. The more profound and enlarging that act of creation is, the more capable it makes us of enriching other aspects of ourselves—both as individuals and as dual participants in that special grace and splendor that exist when we are beings in love.

Afterword

The material in this book involves a consistent application of the concepts of a major philosophical movement of this century—existential phenomenology—to human behavior in general and to human sexuality in particular. The phenomenological movement is based on the work of some of the most important figures of twentieth-century thought: Edmund Husserl, Martin Heidegger, Jean-Paul Sartre, Martin Buber, and Karl Jaspers. In their thinking, the tendency of technological civilization to view human beings as mere assembled objects which can be split into measurable component parts resulted in a fragmentation and depersonalization that was not descriptive of the nature of people as we really experience them or of the world in which we live. The technological concept of humans did not seem to take into proper account the wholeness, the directionality, the ambiguity, and the anxiety of the human condition.

The need for a new way of looking at the nature of human beings was accentuated by the consequences of the industrial and scientific revolutions of the late nineteenth and early twentieth centuries. Matter was being dissolved into energy, as in the terse Einsteinian equation $E = mc^2$. In quantum physics, mathematics, and many other fields, new developments led to a universe that was understood not in terms of exact location and fixed structure, but rather in terms of fluctuation—with a resulting need for a statistical description based on probability. The instability of things thus came to seem definitive.

Similarly, human beings were viewed in the social sciences as creatures manipulated by forces beyond their control, ultimately lacking the ability to choose their own direction in life. What was more, these reductionist, relativistic, and essentially despairing views of humanity were set in the context of the actual crises of Western civilization caused by successive world wars, depression, cataclysmic social destructiveness, and threatening nuclear explosiveness.

To escape from these dead ends of theory and despair, the phenomenologist starts from the top, looking at actual individuals in their concrete life situations, and attempts to perceive the essential relationships of situations and things. Phenomenologists deal with and search for a direct unprejudiced understanding of what is immediately perceived, using the least possible number of suppositions. By starting from the top, instead of breaking everything down into isolated particles that must be rebuilt into a synthetic structure, they allow the integral phenomena of life to speak for themselves in the particular situations and meaningful relationships in which they exist.

For the phenomenologist—indeed for all human beings—objects and people are not neutral, but are always experienced in a meaningful relationship. For example, when different people encounter a tree they do so in different ways, depending on who they are and their special relationship to the tree. A hunter sees the tree as something to hide behind while stalking his quarry. The lumberjack sees the tree as providing potential sources of lumber. The artist approaches the tree in terms of its form, its color, and its place in the overall composition, perceiving a mood that exists in the landscape. A geologist might view the tree as a demonstration of the type of soil in which it grows. And a weary traveler will see the tree as an object that will provide refreshing coolness, a place to rest along the road.

Thus, the immediate meaningful interaction between particular persons and the tree can be apprehended. Being open to the intrinsic perceived pattern of these interactions allows one to understand the individuals in their concrete situations. The stealth of the hunter, the measuring eye of the lumberjack, the slumped posture of the fatigued journeyer seeking shelter all give direct evidence of the nature of the particular relationship that exists between aspects of the tree and the relating individuals.

For several decades I have been working on the utilization of this approach in the fields of psychology, psychiatry, and psychotherapy. In developing the conceptions that underlie my work with patients and my analyses of both sleep positions and sex positions, I owe a debt to three remarkable Swiss psychiatrists and psychoanalysts: Ludwig Binswanger, Gustav Bally, and Medard Boss. Two of these, Bally and Boss, were among my own teachers. I am especially indebted to my mentor and friend Medard Boss for his fundamental contributions to the understanding of the human meaning of the love-sex experience.

I am also indebted to John W. Malone for his editorial assistance in the writing of this book.

About the Author

Samuel Dunkell was graduated from the University of Zurich Medical School in 1954 and did his psychiatric training at Manhattan State and Mt. Sinai hospitals in New York City and his psychoanalytic training at New York's Postgraduate Center for Mental Health, of which he is now Associate Medical Director and Director of Psychiatry. His first book, SLEEP POSITIONS, is also available in Signet paperback.